D1414072

CHOSEN - NOT CURSED!

- Destiny of the Spiritual Ethiopian -

By

Jefferson Edwards

SECOND EDITION

Copyright, © 1989, by Jefferson D. Edwards, Jr., Th.M., Box 300873, Kansas City, MO 64130. All rights reserved. No part of this book may be reproduced in any form without permission in writing from the author. Printed in the United States of America.

Published by Vincom, P.O. Box 702400, Tulsa Ok. 74170, (918)254-1276.

All Scriptures contained herein are from the King James Version of the Bible unless otherwise specified.

ISBN 0-927936-00-3

ACKNOWLEDGEMENTS

My deepest appreciation to my wife, Debra, who has been such an encouragement and inspiration in the writing of this book. Her continuous support and partnership in ministry have enabled me to complete this book quicker than I thought possible.

My thanks go to my previous secretary, Joan Siebert, who so graciously came back on board to transcribe the original tapes of this message and to Elsie Livingston who helped type the first manuscript.

Finally, a special thank you goes to Judson Cornwall, my father in the Gospel, who did a once-over editing of the final manuscript. His comments and suggestions have greatly added to the quality of this book.

DEDICATION

I dedicate this book to the congregation of Inner-City Christian Center, who have stuck with me through thick and thin, who have allowed me to preach and walk out this message with them; and who have helped finance the initial printing of this book. They have participated in the processing of God in making me a pastor and in preparing me to be a voice to the Body of Christ.

TABLE OF CONTENTS

Preface

PREFACE

To be enslaved because of choices made is one thing; to be in bondage because of religious or political convictions is another; but to be born in enslavement just because of our race is preposterous. God never intended that any race of persons automatically be the servants of another race of persons. Still, there are thousands of Christians, many of them black, who have been brainwashed to believe this. This has produced a feeling of superiority in the dominate race with a subsequent feeling of inferiority in the dominated race. Both of these extremes build fortress-like walls that separate and isolate. Although each attitude is false, if reinforced long enough, it will be believed and become a guiding force in life. **"For as he thinks in his heart, so is he"** (Proverbs 23:7) is far more than a wise observation. It is a principle of life.

Jefferson Edwards was reared with a subservient thought pattern, but he rebelled against it. His rebellion didn't change his thoughts or his life, but the deep dealings of God did. When his resentment and anger were flushed from his system, God began to show him the divine purposes He has always had for the black race.

I have not only known Jefferson Edwards for a long time, I have ministered in his church repeatedly. As a matter of fact, I was the best man at his wedding. I have watched this man implement his new-found freedom in his life and ministry, and I have observed how the Lord has used him to help others, both black and white, to reappraise their attitudes toward themselves and others.

This book is the product of his life and ministry. I highly recommend it to anyone, especially the Body of Christ. It will be a revelation to many, a release to some, and a refreshing to us all.

- Judson Cornwall
Phoenix, Arizona - 1989

Chapter 1

Gospel of the Kingdom

And this gospel of the kingdom shall be preached in all the world for a witness unto all nations; and then shall the end come.

- Matthew 24:14

When the Lord first began to speak to me about this verse, I thought only of the Great Commission. In studying this verse further, however, I saw that it related to God's purposes as it pertains to reaching and including every race in His overall plan for the world.

"And this gospel of the kingdom..."

The "Gospel of the Kingdom" is almost a foreign term to many in the black culture. The true meaning of receiving the Gospel of the Kingdom is even more alien.

Kingdom speaks of the sovereign rule and reign of God, the government of God, the dominion of God, and the throne of God.

We must willingly lay down our own rule and reign in order to embrace God's rule and reign. God never will over-power a person's will. The coming of the Kingdom of God into our lives is distinguished by two words: "Not my will, but Thy will be done." The "m" must give way to the "Th."

"...shall be preached in all the world..."

To preach the Gospel in all the world means to preach to five levels: the country, the city, the household, the family, down to each individual person (the temple).

Not only will it require large ministries filling stadiums to preach to the masses and to take the Gospel to all the world, but God has commissioned every believer in the Lord Jesus Christ - of every ethnic group and every color - to share in taking the Gospel of the Kingdom to every part of the world.

"...for a witness..."

The word <u>witness</u> has little to do with our mouths. The Greek word for <u>witness</u> is *marturion*, which means "something evidential or evidence given." <u>Evidential</u> means "affording evidence or clearly proving."

The English words translated from this word are <u>to be testified</u> or <u>testimony</u>. <u>To be testified</u> has nothing to do with our mouths. It has to do with the foundational principle of the New Testament found in John 1:14.

> *And the Word was made flesh, and dwelt among us, (and we beheld his glory, the glory as of the only begotten of the Father,) full of grace and truth.*

It speaks of an evidential lifestyle. The Gospel of the Kingdom, the rule of God, the reign of God, the dominion of God, the government of God, and the throne of God shall be preached in all the world - every country, every city, every household, every family, and ultimately to the individual temple or dwelling place, for a witness or an evidential lifestyle!

Many countries have had salvation preached to them, but they have <u>not</u> had the Gospel of the Kingdom preached as an evidential lifestyle. That is, they haven't had the Gospel of the Kingdom as the "Word made flesh."

Jesus will not return until the members of the black culture have had the Gospel of the Kingdom preached as an evidential lifestyle.

The evidential Kingdom lifestyle must be established in every nation before God will judge contrary lifestyles. There's an old saying, "What you are speaks so loudly that I can't hear what you say." We can reverse this, "What you are speaks so loudly that I hear you."

There must be a witness of God's throne in our lives that comes not only by what we speak with our mouths, but by how we live our lives. Not what we hear, but what we are. Not what we should be, but what we are.

"...unto all nations..."

The word <u>nations</u> is the Greek word <u>ethnos</u>. From this word, we get the English word "ethnic" or "ethnic group." It literally means "a race" (as of the same habit) or "a tribe," specifically foreign (non-Jewish), usually implying a pagan tribe. Some of the English translations of this word are Gentile, heathen, or people.

The Gospel of the Kingdom must be preached as a witness to every race. <u>Is God interested in the races</u>? He most assuredly is! When we say, "God is moving in Indonesia," we don't mean the ungodly government of Indonesia. We mean a race of people or a particular ethnic group identified as Indonesians. When we say, "God is moving in Nigeria," we don't mean in the governmental structure of the country of Nigeria that is under military rule, but in the individual lives of the Nigerians.

The Charismatic movement or renewal was basically a move of the Spirit among white middle-class Americans in suburban and small town areas.

Very few black Americans were affected by this move of the Spirit; neither were other ethnic groups unless they fell in the middle-class status.

God always has centered in on particular races of people. He has time periods or seasons where He brings a visitation to particular races or ethnic groups for His purposes.

God chose the Hebrew race in which to glorify His name. He purposed *"...to make thee high above all nations* [races] *which he hath made, in praise, and in name, and in honour; and that thou mayest be an holy people unto the Lord thy God, as he hath spoken"* (Deuteronomy 26:19).

God chose the Hebrews - the most despised race - as His inheritance to reach all other races.

> *For thou art an holy people unto the Lord thy God: the Lord thy God hath chosen thee to be a special people unto himself, above all the people that are upon the face of the earth.*
>
> *The Lord did not set his love upon you, nor choose you, because ye were more in number than any people; for ye were the fewest of all people.*
>
> *- Deuteronomy 7:6,7*

Of Abraham it was said, "**...in thee shall all families** [races] **of the earth be blessed"** (Genesis 12:3). For a period of time, God lifted the Hebrew race above every other race in order to work His purpose, which would eventually include all other races.

God also sent prophets to specific nations [or races] to deliver a message. When God centers in on a particular race, He brings His government, rule, reign, dominion, and throne to that race.

The Gospel of God's rule and reign must come to the black race in America. When the Gospel of the Kingdom is really preached to our race, it will override every other rule and reign that affects or controls the black race.

God's rule must come to override the rule of evil that causes one-half of black teenage girls to get pregnant with about 100 percent of them never getting married; the rule of evil that causes half of black teenage boys to be arrested before the age of 18, destining them to poor jobs because of a police record, ending up in poverty, crime, or drugs; the rule of evil that has caused nearly half of black families to be headed by women. In some areas, statistics show that approximately 70 percent of black family homes are single parent homes headed by women. Then, too, a large percentage of black young men are killed before the age of 25.

Statistics give the black race no destiny...no future...no expected end. The enemy has cheated us from receiving the true Gospel of the Kingdom because of the separation and racial division in the church. However, we as a black culture, have also been cheated by ourselves for not believing God's Word and for not moving into it and applying it to our everyday lives.

It seems as though Satan said to the black race of people, "Since Simon of Cyrene, the black man, helped Jesus carry the cross (the sin, greed, rebellion, and selfishness of the world), I'm going to keep them under the cross."

This is the kind of Gospel that has been preached to the black culture. It has been more of an endurance contest. It has an echo of, "Hold on. One day it will all get better. We will understand it by and by when we fly away."

It is a kind of "Blues Gospel." That is the reason so many preachers in our culture "moan" their messages! The preaching does not echo victory in the rule and reign of God over conditions and oppression...just a tone of endurance. Until recently, even the songs lacked a note of victory...they lacked the reality of walking in victory through God's Kingdom operative in our lives now.

Though the enemy has tried to keep us under the cross, the true Gospel of the Kingdom will bring us to the other side of the cross that we might partake of the resurrection of the Lord and of His rule and reign now!

It is my belief that God wants to visit the black segment of the Body of Christ as a race of people. He wants to bring us out of the attitude that has been perpetuated on us as second-class Christians who are not really involved in the mainstream of the church world.

He wants to visit us as a people that we might have His solutions for the ills of our society. <u>It is our time to receive visitation</u>. There has not been a major visitation among the black populous since the Azusa Street Revival of 1906. God wants to do a "new thing" in our midst.

We must prepare ourselves to receive of God and hunger and thirst for righteousness so we can be filled (See Matthew 5:6).

In fact, it is time we shake ourselves as a race and believe God's Word above any statistic or any apparent fact we face. All of God's Word is a personal letter to anyone who will believe it and receive it.

Our destiny is spelled out in Jeremiah 29:11-14, and it is time we rise up, believe it, and receive it!

> 'For I know the plans I have for you,' declares the Lord, 'plans to prosper you and not to harm you, plans to give you hope and a future [a destiny].
>
> 'Then you will call upon me and come and pray to me, and I will listen to you.'
>
> 'You will seek me and find me when you seek me with all your heart.' 'I will be found by you,' declares the Lord, 'and will bring you back from captivity.'
>
> (NIV)

Chosen - Not Cursed!

Chapter 2

Gospel of Bondage

Messages about salvation and being "born again" have been heard by the black culture for many years in denominational churches. In fact, every angle of salvation that could be found in the Gospels was preached, but rarely did anyone get saved. When the altar call was given, people came forward, shook the preacher's hand, and began to work in the church. Otherwise, they continued life as usual, but there was no heart change.

Black culture was thoroughly saturated with the Gospel of salvation, yet few messages were given about a Christian lifestyle or Kingdom living for the now.

I personally sat in a black denominational church for years and heard messages about salvation every Sunday. However, I was never instructed how to receive Jesus Christ into my heart. I even played an instrument in the church, and I wept during nearly every service. My tears were accepted as an indication of salvation, but they were tears of conviction.

When you indicated that something was missing in your life, you were told to join the choir, become an usher, or do something in the church. Many people felt they were saved by these "works" in the church or involvement in other activities. What a delusion! If I had died during this time before personally asking Jesus Christ to become my Lord and Savior, I would have gone straight to hell.

These "works" and "activities" caused the people to be religious but not Christlike. It is the hardest thing in the world to reach religious people with the Gospel of the Kingdom of Jesus Christ, because they are so accustomed to these traditions and rituals, which is their idea of true Christianity. To attempt to exhort these people on the importance of a personal relationship with the Lord Jesus Christ was futile in most cases. Such an exhortation was foreign, unneeded, and unheeded.

I believe I would be quite accurate in saying that we (the black culture) had the "gospel of bondage" preached. It is hard to believe that this type of preaching came from the black segment of the church which embraced the Pentecostal movement of 1906 out of the Azusa Street Revival.

The gospel of bondage was full of what I term "clothes line" preaching. It consisted of what to put on: don't wear makeup, no jewelry, wear long dresses, don't do this and don't do that. All of this was done in the name of sanctification and holiness, and holiness seemed to be synonymous with ugliness.

The black segment of the Body of Christ had some manifestations of the Holy Spirit, but they did not experience the liberty of the Spirit. The Word of God says, "...**where the Spirit of the Lord is, there is liberty**" (2 Corinthians 3:17).

For instance, to justify the traditional teaching that women should not wear makeup, they referred to Jezebel. Women who wore makeup were called "Jezebels." This was based on 2 Kings 9:30.

> *And when Jehu was come to Jezreel, Jezebel heard of it; and she painted her face [literally about her eyes], and tired [attired] her head, and looked out at a window.*

This particular Scripture has nothing to do with makeup. If it is sin to paint your eyes (apply that to all women), then the adorning of the head and looking through a window are sins, too!

Another tradition taught for doctrine was that women shouldn't wear pants. This was taken out of context from Deuteronomy 22:5.

> *The woman shall not wear that which pertaineth unto*
> *a man, neither shall a man put on a woman's garment:*
> *for all that do so are abomination unto the Lord thy*
> *God.*

The way I see it, women's pants are women's pants, and men's pants are men's pants! At this particular time, everyone wore robes anyway.

If we adhere to Old Testament law, then we should adhere to another verse in this same chapter.

> *Thou shalt make thee fringes upon the four quarters of*
> *thy vesture, wherewith thou coverest thyself.*
>
> *- Deuteronomy 22:12*

This verse indicates that we are in sin if we don't have fringes on our clothes!

Deuteronomy 21:18-21 says if you have a stubborn and rebellious son who will not obey the voice of his father and mother, even when they have chastened him, they are to bring him to the elders of the city. The men of the city will stone him to death, thus putting away the evil.

Many Christian families today have stubborn and rebellious children, but they don't have them stoned to death by the elders and men of the church.

The point I am trying to make is that if we are going to take one of the laws out of Scripture and teach it as a doctrine, then we are responsible for all of the laws. This is the fallacy of this type of gospel of bondage, which is based on binding people to laws. James 2:10 says, **"For whosoever shall keep the whole law, and yet offend in one point, he is guilty of all."**

The services in many of the black churches have been directed toward an emotional release rather than a reality of Christ and a freedom of the Holy Spirit in our midst. Besides, people under this bondage rarely fellowshipped with people outside of their own circles. They became a law unto themselves. Instead of liberating people through the power of the Holy Spirit, they brought them under the traditions of men.

In order for the government of God to come in our lives, there must be a removal of our own reign, rule, dominion, and government. Two governments cannot reign simultaneously. When the Kingdom of God comes, every other government has to go.

Daniel likened the Kingdom of God to a stone cut out without hands that became an exceeding great mountain (See Daniel 2:45). First of all, it knocked down the images or civilizations of the world, the images of gold, silver, brass, iron and clay. The Kingdom of God is going to come, and everything else is going to have to go. The image became chaff, and then the mountain became an exceeding great mountain (See Daniel 2:31-45).

In the Old Testament, we know that the Kingdom of God is likened to mountains in type. God always mounted a house on top of a great major mountain. There are three major mountains (symbolizing kingdoms) with three major houses on them (symbolizing the church): Mount Gibeon and the house is the Tabernacle of Moses; Mount Zion and the house is the Tabernacle of David; and Mount Moriah and the house is the Temple of Solomon.

It is part of the job of the church to cause the kingdoms of this world to become the Kingdom of God and His Christ (See Revelation 11:15). It is the job of the church to bring down the kingdoms, rules, and governments of the world and exalt God's government. That's why our prayer must be, **"Thy kingdom come. Thy will be done in earth, as it is in heaven"** (Matthew 6:10). For the will of God to be done, His Kingdom must come. His will must be done in earth as it is done in heaven - not done as it is in Baptist, Methodist, Catholic, or Pentecostal circles.

"Thy kingdom come...Thy will be done in earth, as it is in heaven" becomes a prayer of the person who plans to dominate and rule in the heavenlies and has the power to tear down principalities and powers and bondages in the earth!

Chapter 3

Gospel of Denial

Only small splurges of the black culture have heard some degree of the Gospel of the Kingdom, and even the white segment of the church which has had the Gospel has moved in it only within their own comfort zones.

In the Civil Rights marches, people moved in the Biblical knowledge they possessed, but they basically were under fundamental teaching that instructed them in more of what not to believe rather than what to believe.

Most of their time was spent saying, "Don't believe this; don't believe that; stick to the fundamentals and nothing else."

Many of our leaders in the black culture, though they were ministers of the Gospel, did not have divine revelation and prophetic insight. The Bible wasn't an open book to them. They did not know or understand typology. They did not understand the purpose of God from the Old Testament, even though many of them attended Schools of Theology and learned history. They were unable to make the Gospel relevant for their day within a Scriptural context, both spiritually and physically.

Jesus made the Kingdom relevant, because after He said, "...Repent [change your mind]: **for the kingdom of heaven is at hand**" (Matthew 4:17), He then went about demonstrating the Kingdom. In demonstrating the Kingdom, He met the needs of the people where they lived! He brought God's laws, truth, and love to where the people lived. He made the Law, the Prophets, and the Psalms relevant to life during that time.

That's why the people said, "We never heard it like this. He comes, and He doesn't preach like the scribes, those who have memorized Scriptures, teaching from a technical point of view. He teaches as One having authority, as though He knows the God He is talking about."

Jesus brought the Law, the Psalms, and the Prophets into the relevancy of their time because, "The Kingdom of God is at hand." The rule of God is here. Jesus was giving them keys. He was giving them truth that can release the Kingdom of God <u>now</u>! He went about demonstrating something of another Kingdom. He went about demonstrating that He was of another Kingdom, and in that other Kingdom, He had power over things in this kingdom.

This is why He raised the child from the dead, because in this earthly kingdom, you will die, but in the Kingdom of God, you will live forever! He brought the powers of the world to come into this earthly realm.

In this earthly kingdom, people have diseases unto death and they die, but in God's Kingdom, there is healing and divine health. He brought the powers of the world to come into a relevancy <u>now</u>! He bombarded this earthly kingdom with God's Kingdom. He was a manifestation of another world. He was a manifestation of the Kingdom of God. He brought the Gospel into a <u>now</u> existence!

We have talked our way out of the present and have put it into the future - the sweet by and by. Jesus never did that. He took the old dead Law, those old dead songs, and those old dead prophets who they religiously read about in every service, yet did not believe. He brought them into the present, applying them to everyday life. He made practical application of the Scriptures to the people's lives.

He began fulfilling everything the Bible said <u>now</u>! He would do something and say, **"Then was fulfilled that which** was spoken by Jeremy [Jeremiah] the prophet..." (Matthew 27:9).

We are not doing things today **"that it might be fulfilled which was spoken by the prophets."** We are not bringing the Bible into present-day reality as much as we should. Jesus brought it into everyday life!

Few black leaders knew very much about applying the Biblical principles to our daily lives now. Instead, most took a few Scriptures and ranted and raved, giving an emotional release. They did the best they could, and we needed them as leaders because we were under such burdens. They didn't know how to release us into another dimension of power.

They didn't know because they didn't believe half of the Bible. We did not have the Gospel of the Kingdom. We had the gospel of salvation, and we had the gospel of hope. We didn't have the gospel of faith. Our conditions seemed too messed up to believe that God could change them. Our conditions were too far gone to believe that the Kingdom could affect us now. We hoped that "later on" it would change. We marched with a lot of hope, but we didn't march in faith.

That is why our songs were so blue. We did not sing by faith. We sang by hope. You know, **"One day it will all get better."** We preached by hope: **"Trouble doesn't last always."** We sang songs like, **"If you just hold out till tomorrow."**

In the churches I came out of, all the mothers cried when they sang. Then they put a little speed to it, and the young folks started "shouting" (or traditionally called "getting happy") as they sang the songs. We had songs that brought tears to us, but not tears of faith. They were tears that this thing was not going to change, but we could endure. This is all most of our black leaders knew. I am not putting them down, because that is all they knew.

No more than a few years ago, the move that we are now a part of and in fellowship with among white Spirit-filled evangelicals and white Spirit-filled fundamentalists, would not allow blacks in their Bible colleges.

The headquarters of the second largest Pentecostal denomination in the world is located in Springfield, Missouri. Many of their founding leaders came out of the Azusa Street Revival of 1906 in Los Angeles, California, where William Seymour, a black minister, laid hands on these men and ordained them.

Blacks were allowed in some white secular colleges because of government money allocated for them. However, in many situations, the black student's academic load was so heavy, he couldn't make it. This was done intentionally by academic advisors.

In the late 1960's, the black culture began having a church movement. It was later called the Civil Rights Movement. During this same period of time, the Charismatic Movement started in white middle-class Americans. The Spirit of God was poured out upon white middle-class America bringing spiritual renewal. These two factions were the two most extreme opposing forces, because the greatest area of racism was between white middle-class and black middle-class and lower class citizens, primarily because they were competing for the job market and better housing.

Outward racism was not generally expressed by the upper-class whites, because they were not in situations to interact with blacks. Blacks offered no threat to their lifestyle or standard of living. But it was the middle-class whites, the ones who were foremen, who worked alongside other blacks, who openly expressed the most hate toward blacks and competed for jobs and housing.

When God started a church movement among the blacks, it wasn't an indepth spiritual movement, because the blacks knew nothing about the ministry of the Holy Spirit. We did not have a foundation in which the Holy Spirit could operate freely, so it was just a church movement and a rising up from traditional social concepts.

Among white middle-class Americans, however, God poured out His Spirit and opened them up to a fresh visitation among the churches. There could have been a joining together, an ending of the Civil War, and a putting down of racism and prejudice in the church. The Civil War never ended in the hearts and minds of many people, because the church did not assume its role of "reconciliation" and lay the axe of God's Word to the roots of the hate, prejudice, and division that were perpetuated in America.

The segmentation of races could have ended during this time of visitation had they listened to the voice of the Holy Spirit, but it didn't happen. Instead, the church movement among the black culture became a political movement, because the appeal had to go to the government to right some of the wrongs of our society.

Blacks have had a gospel of salvation, a gospel of hope, and a gospel of endurance, but not the Gospel of a present Kingdom.

The black segment of the church that did get the Holy Spirit still did not hear the Gospel of the Kingdom. They received the Holy Spirit and continued to preach the gospel of bondage, the gospel of law and tradition, and the gospel of denial. So among the black ranks, anyone who was Spirit-filled was called sanctified, but they were still in bondage because they didn't know what to do with the Holy Spirit. They were not taught and lacked understanding of the ministry of the Holy Spirit in revealing Christ in His fullness and guiding us into all truth.

There was a lot more emotion which helped to release some of the pressures of living under an oppressed society, but the basic philosophy still was to "hold on." You could dance, sing, and shout, but to be "sanctified" meant "don't wear this, don't wear that, don't go here, and don't go there. Just endure things as they are."

The black culture still has not received the Gospel of the Kingdom in its fullness, and those who have been exposed to it still have a hard time accepting it.

The Gospel of the Kingdom will bring dominion and government into a person's life. It will bring regulation and stability. The King's domain must be established in our lives, yet many refuse the rule of Jesus in their lives, preferring to "do their own thing." As a result of this type of attitude, the order of God is rejected.

The Apostle Paul said:

> *Brethren, my heart's desire and prayer to God for Israel is, that they might be saved. [Saved is sozo in the Greek, which means to be healed, delivered, set free, liberated, and made whole.]*

> *For I bear them record that they have a zeal of God [an excitement and enthusiasm], but not according to knowledge.*

> *For they being ignorant of God's righteousness, and going about to establish their own righteousness, have not submitted themselves unto the righteousness of God.*

> *- Romans 10:1-3*

The majority of the Gospel messages to the black culture have been religious and emotional, but have lacked the power to bring change in people's lives.

The Gospel of the Kingdom (the rule, reign, dominion, government, and throne of God) must be preached in all the world as an evidential lifestyle to every race before the end comes. Because it hasn't yet been preached to the black race, there is no need to take on the "rapture syndrome" and prepare to fly away! We are to occupy and reign with the knowledge and wisdom of God dominating our every thought and action.

It's time for members of the black culture to change our attitude and accept the fact that God wants to visit us and deal with us as a race of people. He visited and dealt with white middle-class Americans in the Charismatic renewal. He brought spiritual renewal among the Catholics. God wants to visit us and deal with us.

In Revelation 5:9 and 7:9, John saw a company of every tongue, every nation, and every people. God is making a nation of nations, but to do this, He must first visit the nations or races just as He visited the Hebrews. I believe the key in giving God the freedom to visit us as a race depends upon black leaders.

Black leaders are only now beginning to accept their heritage in Christ. God is working on black Spirit-filled leaders to get them out of the realm of uncertainty and out from under law into the full provision of His grace.

It is time for revival among the black segment of the church. We need revival. We need to be inspired. We need renewal. We need a visitation from God. We need leaders who see the Lord and have a vision of change, who will preach the Gospel of the Kingdom of God.

Through black leaders who are beginning to realize who they are in Christ, God is bringing the glorious Gospel of His Kingdom to us as a race.

Chapter 4

Gospel of Righteousness

The gospel of denial and the fallacy of it's message is exposed when the gospel of righteousness comes. Hallelujah!

The first principle of the Gospel of the Kingdom is righteousness! Righteousness involves right standing with God and right standing with one another. It means the right wisdom of God and the right wisdom toward one another...right standing with one another, an area in which both black and white cultures need a lot of work.

The spiritual permissiveness of our time has allowed the white segment as well as the black segment of the Body of Christ to get by with, "I am the righteousness of God in Christ, praise the Lord; but I don't care anything about you."

We got by with that for a season, but we need to realize that as evil in the land is waxing worse and worse, God's righteous people need to join forces as a single Body, regardless of color.

Revelation 22:11 says, **"He that is unjust, let him be unjust still: and he which is filthy, let him be filthy still: and he that is righteous, let him be righteous still: and he that is holy, let him be holy still."**

The righteous must become more righteous still. I believe what we have called righteousness is going to undergo a major readjustment, the righteousness of God revealed from faith to faith. Paul wrote:

...I am not ashamed of the gospel of Christ: for it is the <u>power</u> with God unto salvation to every one that believeth; to the Jew first, and also to the Greek [regardless of race].

For therein [the Gospel] is the righteousness of God [right standing of God for the times] revealed from faith to faith: as it is written, The just shall live by faith.

- Romans 1:16,17

The church has gotten by with a vertical realm of righteousness, but has avoided like the plague the horizontal realm of righteousness <u>to one another</u>. It will have to change, for we are to be in right standing with God <u>and</u> right standing with one another. Not just right standing with blacks because you are black, or right standing with whites because you are white.

The time demands that he who is righteous shall become more righteous still. No more phoney religion, for 1 John 4:20 says, **"If a man say, I love God, and hateth his brother, he is a liar: for he that loveth not his brother whom he hath seen, how can he love God whom he hath not seen?"**

God is saying what has always been in the Bible: <u>I am rebuilding the importance of your right standing with each other</u>.

Jesus said:

A new commandment I give unto you, That ye love one another; as I have loved you, that ye also love one another.

By this shall all men know that ye are my disciples, if ye have love one to another.

- John 14:34,35

No one gave the disciples an example of how you love one another, because the Jews thought to <u>love one another</u> meant to love the Jews and not the other races. They were racist against every other nation. God has allowed ignorance and denial for a season, but the time has come that the Gospel must go to every nation, every race, and every tribe of people.

God allowed the Jews to wallow in their own prejudices with in their own cultural boundaries for a season, but then there came a time when, "That wall must come down;" when God commissioned apostles to take the gospel of the good news to the Gentiles - that is, to other races.

I believe we are being awakened to the fact that, no matter what our color, we are to love one another as believers in the Lord Jesus Christ. When God commanded us to love one another, that did not mean love one another if we are black, or if we are white. When the Lord said, **"Have love one to another,"** He was talking to His Church (His Body).

We have had a love that is based upon a love within our own cultural realm or within our comfort zone.

Many blacks, because of a history of slavery, feel uncomfortable around white folks and find it difficult to trust them. Many whites also feel uncomfortable around black folks and find it difficult accepting them. As a result, both blacks and whites have a problem loving each other. Both blacks and whites haven't felt comfortable around people of lower economic levels, so they have ignored them. Then most of us don't feel too comfortable around those who are astute, intellectual, and have some money. We only want to love those who are like us. This has gone on for a season, but I believe it is the hour to love all blood bought and blood washed people of God, regardless of color or status.

When Jesus said to love one another, the Jews apparently still thought He meant, "Have love for the Jews," because at that time, if He had told them, "Have love for the Gentiles," He would have had a tough time getting the Gospel out, for He had given them no revelation of the Gentiles yet. He had only mentioned other sheep in the flock that He was going to gather (See John 10:16).

The Jews did not understand what Jesus meant by that statement. I believe that's why He had to raise up a vehement, short in stature, long-nosed, receding-hairlined, terror-to-the-church, whose name was Paul, in order to break the barriers that had existed for such a long time. The church was not ready for this kind of love...love that took the Gospel to every nation. The Jerusalem church tried to keep the message of the Gospel within Jewish boundaries. They simply did not understand that the Gospel must go to every nation [race].

We as believers today have stayed in our comfort zone long enough. The time demands that we see that God is calling for unity. **"That they all may be one..."** (John 17:21).

God will not turn up the thermostat of glory in the United States any more until we are <u>one</u>! When we are one, then He will give us the glory that He had before the world was.

> *That they all may be one; as thou, Father, art in me, and I in thee, that they also may be one in us: that the world may believe that thou hast sent me.*

> *And the glory which thou gavest me I have given them; that they may be one, even as we are one:*

> *I in them and thou in me, that they may be made perfect in one; and that the world may know that thou hast sent me, and hast loved them, as thou hast loved me.*

> *- John 17:21-23*

The gospel of righteousness is a gospel of unity and love one for another, regardless of race or color.

Chapter 5

Prejudices of the Jews

God knew of the prejudices of the Jews. In fact, the Bible is full of prejudices, God dealing with prejudices, and God dealing with people who didn't like other people.

God will not let you bind the gospel to your idiosyncrasies, your culture, your habits, or your racial boundaries. It must be preached. You can't put this Gospel under your own government and rule, because if you only preach to whom you want, then you are taking the Gospel of God's rule, reign, government, and dominion, and you are putting it under your own rule, reign, government, and dominion. When it is under your rule, you only rule within a certain culture, a certain race, and you only let your rule go to a certain people that you like. The disciples had <u>an attitude of exclusivism</u> when Jesus, after His resurrection, was trying to speak to them about things concerning the Kingdom. They wanted to limit the Kingdom's influence to their own national interest: **"...Lord, wilt thou at this time restore again the kingdom to Israel?"** (Acts 1:6).

You can't take the rule of God and put it under your carnal, cultural, racial, and traditional boundaries.

In the Jerusalem church, the Jews were having a wonderful time, but they were not fulfilling Matthew 24:14. They were not preaching the Gospel of the Kingdom to every creature and to every race. They had become comfortable with the Jews only.

In Acts 1, the risen Christ spoke to the apostles about "things pertaining to the Kingdom of God." With in these 40 days of teaching, the apostles still wanted to limit the scope of the Gospel to their own national, racial, and cultural interests. Jesus told them that they would be **"...baptized with the Holy Ghost not many days hence"** (Verse 5).

The Holy Ghost is the Person who will bring the witness of the Kingdom of God into your life and into the nations. The apostles' reply was, **"...Lord, wilt thou at this time restore again the kingdom to Israel?"** (Verse 6). They missed the whole point, because they were bound and blinded by their own national and racial interests.

Jesus quickly corrected them and told them, **"...ye shall receive power, after that the Holy Ghost is come upon you: and ye shall <u>be</u> witnesses unto me both in Jerusalem, and in all Judaea, and in Samaria** [the people you hate]**, and unto the uttermost part of the earth"** (Verse 8). But the Jews didn't receive this commandment because of bondage to their own national and racial interests.

Apostle Paul - Reconciler of the Races

Paul, after his missionary journey to the Gentiles, came to the Jerusalem church. After his arrival, the leaders said to him, "Come and see this big crowd. See how many of the Jews that were zealous of the law and have turned to the Lord. They know that you preach against the Law of Moses and the tradition of the Jews.

"You are talking about these Gentiles coming to the faith, and you know that we [Jews] don't like that. Jews will kill you over their traditions, so we will tell you what to do. Why don't you go down to the temple where we have a few men who are ready to take a vow. In your vow to the Lord, you have to shave your head, so why don't you join them so they will know that you keep the Law of Moses and then they will accept you.

"We don't want you to disturb our crowd, Paul. We want you to stay within our comfort zones. We want you to preach so we won't lose our crowd. Don't mess it up now. We know that you are a keeper of the Law, but the Jews think you are not, so go ahead and keep the ritual of shaving your head, even though we know you don't like it and think it isn't necessary. Just do it for the sake of diplomacy, and let's be at peace with one another. Don't let anything offend your brother."

They used all the Scriptures they could think of to get Paul to keep their laws and traditions. Paul did it for the sake of diplomacy.

Paul had brought some Greeks with him to Jerusalem, and the Jews thought he took them in with him when he took his vows and thereby defiled the temple. They became so angry that the Jews were going to kill Paul (See Acts 21:17-31). These religious hypocrites tried to kill Paul, because he went beyond the Jews' comfort zone and traditions. He went over their religious boundaries. They weren't ready to hear the full Gospel yet, and they weren't ready to take the Gospel beyond their Jewish traditions. They wanted to enjoy the benefits of the Gospel only within their traditional boundaries.

Paul would not stay within their boundaries. God told Paul that He was delivering him from the people to whom He had sent him (See Acts 26:17).

Before Paul became involved with the Gospel of the Lord Jesus Christ, he was a vehement persecutor of Christians.

Paul was an example of how the Jews had been and how many of them continued to be, though they were not as devout and dedicated as Paul.

Paul had persecuted the church with such force that it stopped the church at Jerusalem in its tracks. It didn't stop them too much, however, because they weren't going anywhere or moving forward! They were comfortable in Jerusalem.

Paul had letters which gave him approval to bind and cast into prison all people who were walking in the way of the Lord. He even held the coats of those who consented to stone Stephen to death. When Stephen cried out his last words, "...**Lord, lay not this sin to their charge,**" (Acts 7:60), Paul (still Saul before his conversion) was affected by Stephen's devotion.

Paul (formerly Saul) didn't want to stand there under conviction, so he escalated his pace in persecuting the church. He had letters from the high priests to persecute anyone who called on the Lord. As Paul brought pressure on the Jerusalem church, the Jews were scared. They scattered, fulfilling what God said: "**And this gospel of the kingdom** [the rule, reign, government, and dominion of God] **shall be preached in all the world** [all the land] **for a witness** [evidential lifestyle] **unto all nations** [races]**; and then shall the end come**" (Matthew 24:14).

God was letting them know: <u>"Don't bind My Kingdom by your racism and prejudices."</u>

Chapter 6

Pressure Advances the Gospel to the Samaritans

And Saul was consenting unto his death. And at that time there was a great persecution against the church which was at Jerusalem; and they were all scattered abroad throughout the regions of Judaea and Samaria, except the apostles.

And devout men carried Stephen to his burial, and made great lamentation over him.

As for Saul, he made havock of the church, entering into every house, and haling men and women committed them to prison.

Therefore they that were scattered abroad went every where preaching the word.

- Acts 8:1-4

God sent His Jewish, Mosaic, Babylonian, starched, law-keeping people to the nation they hated the most. The first people who received the Gospel were the arch-haters of Israel - the Samaritans. The Samaritans were actually half-Jews. They evolved out of a union with the Jews and the Assyrians during Ezra's time.

The Jews and the Samaritans were like some of the blacks and whites in America. They hated each others' guts with a passion, and their hate was a tradition that was passed down, reinforced by stereotypes and fears. Jews hated them so much they were willing to go approximately 50 miles out of their way to avoid any contact with them. They were not going into the village of those dogs. They didn't even want to go through the neighborhood. We have some of this same type of fear and prejudice today.

That's the way freeways are built today in our urban cities, to bypass the black neighborhoods. To get to the other parts of a region, it would have been so simple to go through Samaria, but they went all the way around, down another road that was infested with thieves and vandals. They had to be armed to travel that dangerous road.

This is why Jesus said, **"I must needs go through Samaria"** (John 4:4). As Jesus preached the Gospel, He broke down tradition, racial bondages, and barriers.

At Jacob's well in Samaria, Jesus said to a Samaritan woman, **"...Give me to drink"** (John 4:7). This woman was as prejudiced as the Jews, so she responded to Jesus, **"...How is it that thou, being a Jew, askest drink of me, which am a woman of Samaria? for the Jews have no dealings with the Samaritans"** (John 4:9).

A strong racial tension existed between the Samaritans and the Jews. However, God sent the Jews to the Samaritans (who were half-Jews). They were the first people who received the Gospel after the Jews.

God tried the Jews by sending them to their arch-enemies, the ones they hated the most. He could have sent them to another place, but instead, He sent them to the people against whom they were the most racially prejudiced, preaching the Gospel of the Kingdom. If they could preach the Gospel of the Kingdom purely to those they once hated, they could preach the Gospel to anyone.

Philip - Reconciler to the Samaritans

Before the death of Philip, he preached Christ and the Kingdom message, and God verified the message with signs and wonders. If God hadn't confirmed the message, I doubt if the Jews would have accepted the salvation of the Samaritans. If he did not bring a Kingdom lifestyle and witness, the Jews wouldn't have accepted the Samaritans' conversion.

"For the kingdom of God is not in word, but in power" (1 Corinthians 4:20).

The Civil Rights marches have been large in words, but small in power! Many sermons are lengthy in words, but short in power. Such marches and sermons may prick the conscience, but they do not deal with the heart of racism and prejudice.

Americans were convicted under Dr. Martin Luther King's ministry, but the world doesn't know what to do with conviction. When the world is convicted, they want to get out from under the conviction. If they don't get out from under the conviction, then they want to stop the one who is bringing the conviction. The world doesn't like conviction. It doesn't like to be disturbed.

Conviction is good for the church. The church knows what to do with conviction. When conviction comes, repent and turn from wrongdoing.

Sermonizing won't cut it when dealing with prejudices that are so deep. The division between the Jews and the Samaritans was so deep, there had to be a demonstration of another world. There had to be a demonstration of the power of God. Words weren't enough.

Philip went down to Samaria and there were demons crying with loud voices, and he commanded them to come out. Many were healed of palsy. However, the Jews still were not sure they could accept the Samaritans in the church. A lot of the acceptance in the church had to do with the laying on of hands.

Even though they were saved, to be accepted as a part of the church, they had to receive laying on of hands, which is a principle of Scripture. Peter and John, the apostles, had to come down and seal them. Their question was, "Are you really converted?" It was quite an event for them to lay their hands on the Samaritans, because of the strong racial tension between them.

In contrast, in the house of Cornelius, the Gospel was preached and the Holy Ghost came upon them without the laying on of hands (Acts 10:44-45). I believe God sent the Jews to Samaria and had them touch the Samaritans, because He was breaking down barriers that had been built up for thousands of years. When the apostles came down to Samaria, the Samaritans were filled with the Holy Ghost. They received the same witness.

God wants the Gospel of the Kingdom preached to every race for a witness. He meant for the Gospel to go beyond Jerusalem.

Chapter 7

Gospel Then Goes to the Ethiopians - The Black Culture

The second group of people to receive the Gospel was the Ethiopians, a black race of people. Ethiopia is the cradle of the black race. The black race comes out of Cush, the son of Ham (Genesis 10). In many places in the Bible, the Ethiopian is translated "Cushite" or black. Before looking at a portion of the black history in the Bible, I am compelled to share a glimpse of a personal vision which I had.

I went down into hell and entered a room marked, "B.D.," which stood for black destiny. I went in there, found a record of our destiny and brought it out. I found a record of the destiny of a people which Satan has tried his best to hide and destroy. I found that our black destiny is connected to the destiny of all people, because we came out of the same family and we have a part that relates to all of Noah's children.

There is a destiny for the black race. Of the four rivers in Eden, one of those rivers went to Ethiopia, while one of the other rivers went to Havilah.[†] Both are black nations and regions.

From the beginning of time, the black culture has had a spiritual destiny, though it has been clouded and hidden.

The Ethiopians were a prestigious race and a powerful race because of their skill as warriors. They had a natural sense of destiny.

† International Standard Bible Encyclopedia, Vol. 2, p. 1345.

They were neighbors to the Jews for thousands of years. There was little malice between the Jews and the Ethiopians, for they had a good relationship. They were on friendly terms.

Through periods of history, the Ethiopians and the Jews were very close, and they were on the same level of respect and achievement (See 2 Chronicles 12). At times Israel looked up to Ethiopia for their hope and deliverance, because Ethiopia had such strong armies in allegiance with Egypt and Lybia, both African nations.

Then during King Asa's reign (See 2 Chronicles 14), Ethiopia rose up against Judah when Judah and Israel were divided. King Asa, with the help of God, won a great victory over Ethiopia (See 2 Chronicles 14:9-15). From that time forth, Ethiopia was under tribute to Israel and their status as co-equal was changed. They became more of a subservient country to Israel. Before that, they were on good terms with Israel. Throughout Jewish history, the Ethiopians were present in Israel's history.

The entire land of Canaan was inhabited by dark-skinned people. Canaan and Cush were sons of Ham. Ham was the father of the dark-skinned race, and the black race evolved through his son, Cush. Ham means "hot or dark, colored or swarthy." The Hebrew word for Ham is "hot," and is prophetic of the climates that have created the blackness of skin of the Negro and the dark complexions of other people from the same stock.

Egypt is called **"...the land of Ham"** (Psalm 105:23). The Egyptian word for Ham means "black and warm." From Ham we have the Egyptians, Africans, Babylonians, Philistines, and Canaanites. The land of Canaan, which was promised to Israel, was a land of dark-skinned inhabitants.

When Israel inhabited the land of Canaan, it was a fulfillment of the curse pronounced on Canaan by Noah. In fact, there is a controversial issue that relates to what is called "the curse of Ham." Many teachers, secular and religious, have said that blacks are in the lower levels of society and continue to be an oppressed faction because they are under the "curse of

Ham" to be "servants." This is another lie from Satan that justifies oppression and continues to perpetuate racism. The curse was on <u>Canaan</u>, not Ham. **"And he [Noah] said, Cursed be <u>Canaan</u>; a servant of servants shall he be unto his brethren"** (See Genesis 9:25). The indignation of Noah found expression in the thrice repeated curse upon <u>Canaan</u> (Genesis 9:25-27).

The curse of servitude was fulfilled in Joshua's conquest of the Canaanites and their land when he made them hewers of wood and drawers of water.

> *Now therefore ye are cursed, and there shall none of you be freed from being bondmen, and hewers of wood and drawers of water for the house of my God.*

> *And Joshua made them that day hewers of wood and drawers of water for the congregation, and for the altar of the Lord, even unto this day, in the place which he should choose.*

> *- Joshua 9:23,27*

The fact that God gave Israel the land of the Canaanites was a fulfillment of the curse on Canaan to be servants. The black-skinned race came through Ham's eldest son, Cush, which means "black" or "Ethiopian."

Moses Trained by Father-in-law, Jethro

In Exodus 2:11-15, we read:

> *And it came to pass in those days, when Moses was grown, that he went out unto his brethren, and looked on their burdens: and he spied an Egyptian smiting an Hebrew, one of his brethren.*

> *And he looked this way and that way, and when he saw that there was no man, he slew the Egyptian, and hid him in the sand.*

Moses saw things that were wrong, but he tried to bring deliverance in his own strength. <u>The wrath of man never works the righteousness of God, and hate never glorifies God.</u>

And when he went out the second day, behold, two men of the Hebrews strove together: and he said to him that did the wrong, Wherefore smitest thou thy fellow [brother]?

And he said, Who made thee a prince and a judge over us? intendest thou to kill me, as thou killedst the Egyptian? And Moses feared, and said, Surely this thing is known.

Now when Pharaoh heard this thing, he sought to slay Moses. But Moses fled from the face of Pharaoh, and dwelt in the land of Midian [a land associated with Ethiopia]: and he sat down by a well.

Why did Moses flee from the face of Pharaoh? This was actually part of his destiny. God sent him to the land of the Midianites, who were a faction of the Ethiopians, and he sat down by a well. God put Moses in contact with the hierarchy of the Ethiopian tribe (or a faction of the Midianites), of whom Jethro was the priest or the chief.

Now the priest of Midian had seven daughters: and they came and drew water, and filled the troughs to water their father's flock.

And the shepherds came and drove them away: but Moses stood up and helped them, and watered their flock.

And when they came to Reuel [another name for Jethro] their father, he said, How is it that ye are come so soon today?

And they said, An Egyptian delivered us out of the hand of the shepherds, and also drew water enough for us, and watered the flock.

And he said unto his daughters, And where is he? why is it that ye have left the man? call him, that he may eat bread.

And Moses was content to dwell with the man: and he gave Moses Zipporah his daughter.

- Exodus 2:16-21

Of course, Moses was content to dwell with the man, because he was in the desert and he was hungry! Zipporah was a shepherdess or what we would term a woman pastor! Every spiritual truth must find a natural truth for it. If there are no shepherdesses in the Bible, we should have no shepherdesses in the church today, but there were shepherdesses then, and spiritually, there are shepherdesses now.

> *And she bare him a son, and he called his name Gershom [which means "a stranger in a strange land"]: for he said, I have been a stranger in a strange land.*
>
> *And it came to pass in process of time, that the king of Egypt died: and the children of Israel sighed by reason of the bondage, and they cried, and their cry came up unto God by reason of the bondage.*

- Exodus 2:22,23

Moses remained for forty years in the land of Midian (descendants of Abraham & Keturah) with Jethro and his people, an Ethiopian tribe. He became involved in a culture contrary to his. By the time Moses came out of the land of Midian, he thought like an Ethiopian and probably looked like one! It was during those forty years that Moses was processed to be a shepherd, a leader, a deliverer, and a lawgiver. This was part of the life experience that he needed in order to be ready to deliver God's people out of Egypt.

The Ethiopians added much to the destiny of Moses in getting him prepared to go back and free the Lord's people from bondage. They helped lay the foundation for his leadership as a deliverer. Moses was eighty years old now and thought to be mature. All his childish behavior was gone, and he was ready for God's business.

God had directed Moses to go to Jethro and be taught how to serve! Jethro was a wise man, and Moses learned under him.

Jethro's name actually means "excellency." God wanted to impart to Moses a "spirit of excellency" through this black man.

Jethro was a black Ethiopian priest (Numbers 12:1). He was a very honored man as well as Moses' father-in-law. Remember, he took care of Moses in the desert. Moses was in submission to Jethro and apparently respected him. When Moses saw the burning bush, recognized the voice and call of God, and went to answer the call, he asked permission of Jethro to go in response to the call. Jethro told him to go and answer the call of God to deliver the people from Egypt.

> *And Moses went and returned to Jethro his father in law, and said unto him, Let me go, I pray thee, and return unto my brethren which are in Egypt, and see whether they be yet alive.*
>
> *And Jethro said to Moses, Go in peace.*
>
> *- Exodus 4:18*

When Moses returned after the great deliverance from Egypt to the mountain of God and camped, Jethro came to the camp from his own land. Jethro led Moses and the leaders to offer a sacrifice and have a feast in eating before the Lord. In other words, Jethro knew the Lord already and led them to sacrifice to God when Moses came to the wilderness. He was an honored man among the Israelites.

God's Covenant Through Moses With the Ethiopians

Ethiopia has always been close to Israel, first of all, because the lawgiver (Moses) married an Ethiopian woman, and his father-in-law, Jethro, was an Ethiopian priest in the land of Midian.

Moses' father-in-law, Jethro, was a black man. It was Jethro who gave Moses counsel by which Israel's government should be set up (See Exodus 18). Nations throughout history have set up this same form of order within their own boundaries.

Before searching Scriptures, I thought that Moses left his first wife because she didn't want to have their children circumcised, so he married again, but this was not accurate. Moses' only wife was Jethro's daughter.

Moses' wife, the Ethiopian woman whose name was Zipporah, was one of the seven daughters of Jethro. Zipporah was a shepherdess (Numbers 12:1).

Miriam and Aaron were angry because of Moses marrying a black woman. They were not pleased with Moses' choice of a mate.

> *And Moses said unto Hobab, the son of Raguel [another name for Jethro or Jether], the Midianite [also called Kenite, meaning of black or Ethiopian descent], Moses' father in law, we are journeying unto the place of which the Lord said, I will give it you: come thou with us, and we will do thee good: for the Lord hath spoken good concerning Israel.*
>
> *- Numbers 10:29*

To whom was Moses talking? To his father-in-law, who was an Ethiopian. They were not even settled in the land, but Moses took another tribe with him.

> *And he said unto him, I will not go; but I will depart to mine own land, and to my kindred.*
>
> *- Verse 30*

In other words, Jethro said, "I have an inheritance myself, so I will not go."

> *And he [Moses] said, Leave us not, I pray thee; forasmuch as thou knowest how we are to encamp in the wilderness, and thou mayest be to us instead of eyes.*
>
> *- Verse 31*

Jethro and his people travelled in the wilderness, feeding their flocks. Thus, Moses was saying, "You, Jethro, will be our guiding light, for you know the wilderness area through which we will be travelling."

And it shall be, if thou go with us, yea, it shall be, that what goodness the Lord shall do unto us, the same will we do unto thee.

- Verse 32

Moses was saying that the promises to Israel were the same promises to the Ethiopians. That's why the Gospel had to go to the Jews, the Samaritans (half-Jews), and then to the Ethiopians.

First, God dealt with the racism of the Jews toward the Samaritans (half-Jews). God basically wanted them to know that this Gospel would break down their racist attitudes. He wanted them to go to the ones they hated the most, and take His love and His Kingdom to them. They had to allow His Kingdom to override their will.

For God's Kingdom to come into all the ends of the earth, we must override our personal wills. Many times we don't get God's government, because we don't want to let go of our wills.

Often, God will cause us to go, first of all, to those against whom we are most prejudiced, our greatest barrier, and then He will cause us to go to the ones who have been the least among us. Such was the case when the Jews took the Gospel to the Ethiopians.

One Ethiopian Receives a Visitation From Philip Through Four Divine Interventions

God took Philip out of a great revival to a desert to minister the Gospel of the Kingdom to one black man and preach Christ! Just think of it! One man, and this man was an Ethiopian!

The eighth chapter of Acts speaks of an Ethiopian sitting in his chariot reading the Law. You may be thinking, "What is an Ethiopian doing with the Law? That was the Jews' religion. That was Israel's religion. How did the Ethiopian get the Law?" Folks, Ethiopians were as versed in the Law as the

Jews, because they were present when the lawgiver [Moses] gave the law.

God had kept covenant with the Jews, and God was about to keep covenant with the Ethiopians (Kenites). The Jews were involved with covenant through the law of Moses and through the teachings of the prophets so they were in candidacy for the grace that came by Jesus Christ. **"For the law was given by Moses, but grace and truth came by Jesus Christ"** (John 1:17). Both the Jews and the Ethiopians had received the law that came by Moses. Black Ethiopians were right there when Moses gave the law. Moses was married to the Ethiopian woman, Zipporah, and Jethro, his father-in-law, and his family were present to receive the law from Moses.

Moses' relationships give valid support to the presence of a faction of the Ethiopians being constantly involved with the Jews and the law. Therefore, the law had come by Moses basically to the Jews and the Ethiopians. Because of this fact, the Ethiopians had a right to receive the good news of the Gospel of Jesus Christ, because they had already been fulfilled in receiving the law of Moses. That's why the Ethiopian eunuch was reading from the book of Isaiah. He was familiar with the law, as Ethiopians had been for hundreds of years, or since the days of Moses.

The Ethiopian eunuch had also come to Jerusalem to worship during one of the times that male Jews were required in the law to come and worship (See Acts 8:27b; Exodus 34:23,24; and Deuteronomy 16:16).

God had purposed to use this one Ethiopian eunuch, who was already fulfilled in the law, to now receive "grace and truth" that came by Jesus Christ. God was fulfilling His nature as a "covenant-keeping God" and releasing a "destiny of purpose" to "Spiritual Ethiopia," the black segment of the Body of Christ.

The sacred account of Philip's visitation to the Ethiopian is in Acts 8:26-39.

God allowed four miraculous acts of divine intervention to make sure one Ethiopian received the Gospel. The advancement of the Gospel beyond the Jews went first to the Samaritans and then to the Ethiopian eunuch. The circumstances beyond the general persecution by which the Ethiopian eunuch received the Gospel of the Kingdom of God are very unique. It involved <u>four divine interventions</u>.

First Intervention

The first intervention was angelic: **"And the <u>angel of the Lord</u> spake unto Philip..."**

God sent a special messenger to tap Philip on the shoulder and say, "Philip, I have something for you to do." Angelic intervention was to make sure Philip met his appointment with God. The angel of the Lord said, **"...Arise, and go toward the south unto the way that goeth down from Jerusalem unto Gaza, which is <u>desert</u>"** (Verse 26). God specifically said that it was "desert." This is important, since one of the reasons Moses made a covenant with the Kenites (a faction of the Ethiopians) was because they knew the wilderness <u>and</u> the desert.

Moses' father-in-law, an Ethiopian priest, knew the desert. Moses said, "You shall be <u>eyes</u> to keep us in the way. You will have special sight in the wilderness."

I believe a special sight will come to the "spiritual Ethiopians" (the black race) in this hour to <u>see</u> the things of God. We, as a black race, have been handicapped and looked upon as second-class Christians for too long. We have not been as "eyes" for the Church in the wilderness journeyings of life. But God is going to grant us insight in this hour that we may become "spiritual eyes" to the Body of Christ.

God is a God of equity, and I am convinced that in this hour He will override the prejudice and racism by giving <u>strategic insight</u> to godly men and women of the black culture.

Moses said, "You will be eyes to us in the wilderness," and in this particular Scripture, the "wilderness" is the same thing as a "desert."

This Ethiopian had no problem in the desert. He was resting and reading in the desert while en route to his home. He knew where he was going. He wasn't lost. He just stopped in the desert to read the Word.

But the angel said to Philip, **"Arise...I'm going to show you where to go."** Philip did not know where he was going. He had been in a great revival in Samaria, and the angel redirected his steps. For God to divinely redirect Philip by the intervention of an angel, you can be sure this was of utmost importance to God's purposes.

Verse 27 says, **"And he** [Philip] **arose and went..."** Thank God for an obedient deacon who took on the anointing of the apostles of God! **"...and, behold, a man of Ethiopia, an eunuch of great authority under Candace queen of the Ethiopians..."** (Verse 27). This Ethiopian Jew was in Jerusalem for one of the three feasts. He was there visiting under the instructions of the Law, coming to worship God at the required feast.

This Ethiopian knew the God of Moses. He knew the God of the Law. Therefore, he was in a good position to know the Son of God, who came in fulfillment of the Law. He was not just an ordinary servant. He was a servant with authority, who had the charge of all Queen Amanitere's treasure. He was the Secretary of the Treasury of Ethiopia. He was a man of wisdom who could handle wealth. He was a diplomat and **"...had come to Jerusalem for to worship"** (Verse 27).

It is possible that the eunuch was a descendant of Moses' wife, because she was an Ethiopian. The Ethiopians were right there. When the Law was read, there was a company of Kenites, a faction of the Ethiopians, present to hear the Law.

Verse 28 continues, **"Was returning, and sitting in his chariot read Esaias the prophet."** To have a chariot was like having a Cadillac. The eunuch was not riding on an old donkey or a mule! He was in a chariot. That meant he had money and stature.

Second Intervention

Let's read about the second divine intervention involving the Holy Spirit speaking. **"Then the Spirit said unto Philip, Go near, and join thyself to this chariot..."** (Verse 29). The Holy Spirit spoke to Philip to get involved with the Ethiopian eunuch.

No doubt Philip would have passed on by the eunuch, but the Spirit said, "This is why you are here...this is the man."

> *And Philip ran thither to him, and heard him read the prophet Esaias, and said, Understandest thou what thou readest?*
>
> *And he said, How can I except some man should guide me? And he desired Philip that he would come up and sit with him.*
>
> *- Verses 30,31*

It must have been a grand chariot for Philip to join the Ethiopian in it.

> *The place of the scripture which he read was this, He was led as a sheep to the slaughter; and like a lamb dumb before his shearer, so opened he not his mouth.*
>
> *In his humiliation his judgment was taken away: and who shall declare his generation?*
>
> *- Verses 32,33*

Someone in humility and in judgment is going to declare His generation. This speaks of the lifestyle of the black community. **"...for his life is taken from the earth"** (Verse 33). Who is going to, in humility and judgment, continue to declare Jesus Christ to their generation? Who will declare His day of visitation?

And the eunuch answered Philip, and said, I pray thee, of whom speaketh the prophet this? of himself, or of some other man?

Then Philip opened his mouth, and began at the same scripture, and preached unto him Jesus.

- Verses 34,35

The Law, the Psalms, and the prophets all reveal Jesus Christ.

Third Intervention

The third intervention involved a divine supply of water. **"And as they went on their way, they came unto a certain water..."** (Verse 36).

The Ethiopian was in the desert, so what is enough water to be baptized in doing in the desert? God was keeping covenant.

The following Scriptures substantiate the covenant-keeping nature of God as it relates to having an appointment with this Ethiopian eunuch in the wilderness of the desert.

Know therefore that the Lord thy God, he is God, the faithful God, which keepeth covenant and mercy with them that love him and keep his commandments to a thousand generations.

- Deuteronomy 7:9

He hath given meat [will or purpose] unto them that fear him: he will ever be mindful of His covenant.

He hath shewed his people the power of his works, that he may give them the heritage of the heathen.

- Psalm 111:5,6

I the Lord have called thee in righteousness, and will hold thine hand, and will keep thee, and give thee for a covenant of the people, for a light of the Gentiles;

To open the blind eyes, to bring out the prisoners from the prison, and them that sit in darkness out of the prison house.

I am the Lord: that is my name: and my glory will I not give to another, neither my praise to graven images.

Behold, the former things are come to pass, and new things do I declare: before they spring forth I tell you of them.

Sing unto the Lord a new song, and his praise from the end of the earth, ye that go down to the sea, and all that is therein; the isles, and the inhabitants thereof.

Let the wilderness and the cities thereof lift up their voice, the villages that Kedar doth inhabit: let the inhabitants of the rock sing, let them shout from the top of the mountains.

Let them give glory unto the Lord, and declare his praise in the islands.

- Isaiah 42:6-12

Verse 11 says, **"Let the <u>wilderness</u>...lift up their voice, the villages that Kedar doth inhabit..."** Kedar is a dark-skinned or black race. Kedar is the son of Ishmael, who was the son of Abraham and Hagar, the Egyptian (African). These were dark-skinned people who dwelt in the East country.

Another covenant passage is found in Isaiah 43:19-21:

Behold, I will do a new thing; now it shall spring forth; shall ye not know it? I will even make a way in the <u>wilderness,</u> and rivers in the <u>desert.</u>

The beast of the field shall honour me, the dragons and the owls: because I give waters in the <u>wilderness,</u> and

Chosen - Not Cursed!

rivers in the desert, to give drink to my people, my chosen.

Do you think the Ethiopian eunuch was chosen? Definitely! It is demonstrated by four divine interventions.

This people have I formed for myself; they shall shew forth my praise.

This Ethiopian was the chosen of God, and God brought him waters in the wilderness and rivers in the desert. His purpose is for "Spiritual Ethiopia" to show forth His praise.

Look at Isaiah 40:3. "The voice of him that crieth in the wilderness, Prepare ye the way of the Lord, make straight in the desert a highway for our God."

Now, let's look at Isaiah 41:17-20:

When the poor and needy seek water, and there is none, and their tongue faileth for thirst, I the Lord will hear them, I the God of Israel will not forsake them.

I will open rivers in high places, and fountains in the midst of the valleys: I will make the wilderness a pool of water, and the dry land springs of water.

I will plant in the wilderness the cedar, the shittah tree, and the myrtle, and the oil tree; I will set in the desert the fir tree, and the pine, and the box tree together;

That they may see, and know, and consider, and understand together, that the hand of the Lord hath done this, and the Holy One of Israel hath created it.

What is so important about these trees? These trees grow in different regions in their own natural habitat. One grows in the North, one in the South, one in the East, and the other in the West. God says He will plant them all together.

We are likened unto trees planted. God wants to bring us together from all kinds of diverse races, cultures, and backgrounds as a testimony of the glory of God.

*That they all may be one; as thou, Father, art in me,
and I in thee, that they also may be one in us: that the
world may believe that thou hast sent me.*

*And the glory which thou gavest me I have given them;
that they may be one, even as we are one:*

*I in them, and thou in me, that they may be made
perfect in one; and that the world may know that thou
hast sent me, and hast loved them, as thou hast loved
me.*

- John 17:21-23

This Ethiopian was a man from Africa in the desert of
Israel. He was one of those trees that God planted in the desert
and brought water to give drink to His chosen, because the
Ethiopian was chosen to have a part in this same lot with the
Jews. He was one of those strange trees that should not have
been in the desert, but there he was!

"Then the Spirit said unto Philip, Go near..." (Acts 8:29).
The Holy Spirit told Philip, "There's a tree I want to plant in My
vineyard in the desert. I am bringing a root out of the dry
ground!"

Here was a strange tree. God is going to bring up a lot of
strange trees and plant them in His house. He will make them
trees of divine purpose.

Fourth Intervention

The fourth divine intervention is found in Acts 8:39. **"...the
Spirit of the Lord caught away Philip..."**

*And as they went on their way, they came unto a
certain water: and the eunuch said, See, here is water;
what doth hinder me to be baptized?*

*And Philip said, If thou believest with all thine heart,
thou mayest. And he answered and said, I believe that
Jesus Christ is the Son of God.*

Chosen - Not Cursed!

And he commanded the chariot to stand still [that means that he had someone else driving the chariot]: and they went down both into the water [he did not sprinkle], both Philip and the eunuch; and he baptized him.

And when they were come up out of the water, the Spirit of the Lord caught away Philip...

- Verses 36-39

God led Philip to the Ethiopian eunuch by an angel, and He took him away by His Spirit. This is the only account in the New Testament of someone divinely transported other than that of Jesus Christ. It involved getting the Gospel to the Ethiopian.

...that the eunuch saw him no more: and he went on his way rejoicing.

But Philip was found at Azotus: and passing through he preached in all the cities, till he came to Caesarea [Philippi - that's where he lived].

- Verses 39,40

These are the four divine interventions involved in bringing the Gospel to this Ethiopian eunuch. God called Philip away from a great revival in Samaria and used him to cross the boundaries of two different cultures. First, the Jews who hated the Samaritans, and then the Ethiopians who were in bondage to the Jews. We need to give applause to Philip, because God used him to transcend those cultures. Of course, we know that Peter and John came down and laid their hands upon the Samaritans after they had received Christ, but to get to this one black man involved divine intervention.

<u>Philip went to Samaria because of the persecution in Jerusalem, but he went to the desert because an angel spoke to him</u>. The Spirit of the Lord told him to join with the eunuch. Then there was a divine intervention of water being found in the desert, then the catching away of Philip. Four miracles involving one man. God had a purpose. God had something

that had to be accomplished. There was a divine destiny that had to be fulfilled.

"Endich, as tradition names him, was the Ethiopian eunuch, whom Philip, the deacon of Jewish ancestry, converted and baptized."[1]

From the very beginning, the Ethiopians were a part of God's chosen people. Jethro was honored when he came to see Moses. Then Jethro called a feast before the Lord, because he was a priest of the One True God, and he offered sacrifices unto God. All the elders had a feast, and they ate before the Lord.

Jethro knew God for himself. There was an influence of the Law upon black Ethiopians from the very beginning, because God joined two nations when Moses married Zipporah, an Ethiopian. Moses made a covenant: "...what **goodness** the **Lord shall do unto us, the same will we do unto thee**" (Numbers 10:32).

We must understand this, because it is tied to the destiny of the black segment of the Body of Christ. As I shared with you earlier in a vision, I went down into hell and opened the files which were called "secret." They were top secret. But I got right in there and looked. I took the camera of the Holy Ghost and started taking pictures in the top secret files. It is all over my heart now and has become part of my very being. I went in that spiritual dimension and found a record of the destiny of black people.

Black culture has a place in God's purposes. So much negative teaching from history has been taught to blacks, telling them that we are not a people of purpose. We have a purpose in God, not just because we are black, but because "righteousness that exalts a race" has come to us, first being witnessed in the Law. But in the Law, neither the Jews nor the Ethiopians could obtain righteousness. But in Christ and by the Gospel of the Kingdom we not only witness righteousness, but we obtain it. "**For he hath made him to be sin for us, who**

---

1   Holly, Alonzo Potter. God and the Negro, p. 102.

knew no sin; that we might be made the righteousness of God in him" (2 Corinthians 5:21). "But of him are ye in Christ Jesus, who of God is made unto us...righteousness..." (1 Corinthians 1:30).

His purposes are revealed to us in Christ Jesus, just as they are revealed to anyone of any color who will submit to His lordship.

The involvement of the Ethiopian was a part of the history of Israel from its beginnings. That's why the Ethiopian was sitting in his chariot reading the Law. Ethiopians knew and were accustomed to the Law, for they were present when it was given.

Chapter 8

The Queen of Sheba

Involved With the Jews

A n Ethiopian queen, Queen Makeda, is identified in the Bible as the Queen of Sheba.

The Queen of Sheba (Makeda) is also known among the Ethiopians as "Dawn-Upon-the-Land" and "The-Panther-in-the-Blossom." According to the Kebra Nagast ("The Glory of Kings," an ancient Ethiopian chronicle), her reign was one of a series wherein only females reigned, and each was a virgin.[2]

"Sheba was not in Africa, where Ethiopia is today, but in Southern Arabia in the area that corresponds to Yemen today. It was a wealthy trading nation. Some time after the days of Solomon, the Sabeans became the most important people of Southern Arabia. They were great engineers as well as traders. They built large dams and extensive irrigation systems that helped to create what history has called Arabia Felix, 'Happy Arabia.'

"Between the tenth and seventh centuries B.C., the Sabeans colonized Axum, across the Red Sea on the coast of Africa. Axum conquered the Biblical Ethiopia, or Cush, and is forerunner of modern Ethiopia. Here is the linkage then between Sheba in Arabia and Ethiopia in Africa. If a Solomonic heritage for Haile Selassie is true, it must have been traced

---

2   Woolsey, Raymond H. Men and Women of Color in the Bible, p. 52.

through a monarchial transfer from one coast of the Red Sea to the other. Perhaps there was a period when the Sabean reign covered both coasts simultaneously."[3] It is also quite possible that during this time period, the Red Sea was not as broad and long in its coasts, thereby minimizing the separation between the two coasts.

"Judah and Israel were more in tune with the people to their south and east than they were with the Egyptians and Mesopotamians. They had come into Canaan from that direction; the Edomites were called their 'brothers' and the Moabites and Ishmaelites were their 'cousins.' There were no geographical barriers between them and trade was freer. In Baruch 3:23 the Arabians are called the 'Sons of Hagar,' and the book of Psalms refers to the Hagarenes or Hagarites (Psalm 83:6,7)."[4]

Not often recognized is the important part that black people and a particular black man played in the construction of Solomon's Temple. We refer to Hiram, king of Tyre.

"Hiram had been a close friend of David. When the latter was building his palace in Jerusalem, Hiram had supplied cedar from the renown forests of Lebanon. Now, Solomon made arrangements for more supplies for the building of the Temple. Solomon supplied laborers to work with Hiram's skilled timbermen for the felling of cedar and fir. The logs were floated in great rafts down the seacoast to a spot near Jerusalem and taken overland to the Temple. Hiram's men—Phoenicians, descendants of Canaan—also worked with Solomon's skilled stonemasons for the preparations of the huge stones that went into the Temple walls. The workmanship was so carefully done at the quarry that when they were put into place in the Temple, not a sound of chisel or hammer was heard."[5]

"Makeda's empire traded with Africa, India, and Palestine. She had a merchant marine consisting of seventy-three ships

---

3   Ibid., p. 51.
4   Ibid., p. 51.
5   Ibid., p. 50.

and large camel caravans that traveled to Axum and Aswan and Assyria. Gold was a chief commodity, as well as spices, precious stones, and salt."[6]

"When Solomon was building the temple, he sent messages to all the merchants of the four corners of the world to bring him what he required and he would pay them in gold and silver. Among the merchants who responded to the call was Tamrin, the merchant of Makeda, the Queen of Ethiopia (or Sheba), who brought red gold, sapphire, and black wood that could not be eaten by worms. He was struck with amazement at the splendor of Solomon's kingdom and the wisdom of Solomon himself and brought back such a marvelous report of him to the queen that she determined to visit him herself."[7]

> And when the queen of Sheba heard of the fame of Solomon concerning the name of the Lord, she came to prove him with hard questions.
>
> And she came to Jerusalem with a very great train, with camels that bare spices, and very much gold, and precious stones: and when she was come to Solomon, she communed with him of all that was in her heart.
>
> And Solomon told her all her questions: there was not any thing hid from the king, which he told her not.
>
> And when the queen of Sheba had seen all Solomon's wisdom, and the house that he had built,
>
> And the meat of his table, and the sitting of his servants, and the attendance of his ministers, and their apparel, and his cupbearers, and his ascent by which he went up unto the house of the Lord; there was no more spirit in her.
>
> And she said to the king, It was a true report that I heard in mine own land of thy acts and of thy wisdom.

---

6   Ibid., p. 52.
7   Jones, A. H. M. and Monroe, Elizabeth. A History of Abyssinia, p. 10,11.

Howbeit I believed not the words, until I came, and mine eyes had seen it: and, behold, the half was not told me: thy wisdom and prosperity exceedeth the fame which I heard.

Happy are thy men, happy are these thy servants, which stand continually before thee, and that hear thy wisdom.

Blessed be the Lord thy God, which delighted in thee, to set thee on the throne of Israel: because the Lord loved Israel for ever, therefore made he thee king, to do judgment and justice.

And she gave the king an hundred and twenty talents of gold, and of spices very great store, and precious stones: there came no more such abundance of spices as these which the queen of Sheba gave to king Solomon.

And the navy also of Hiram, that brought gold from Ophir, brought in from Ophir great plenty of almug trees, and precious stones.

And the king made of the almug trees pillars for the house of the Lord, and for the king's house, harps also and psalteries for singers: there came no such almug trees, nor were seen unto this day.

And king Solomon gave unto the queen of Sheba all her desire, whatsoever she asked, beside that which Solomon gave her of his royal bounty. So she turned and went to her own country, she and her servants.

- 1 Kings 10:1-13

"First enumerated among the gifts that the Queen of Sheba brought to Solomon is spices. This reflects the fact that the chief element in the economy of South Arabia was the production and distribution of frankincense and myrrh. The only archeological artifacts found in Palestine that derive from Arabia are incense burners and a clay stamp relating to the frankincense trade. (The name of Abraham's second wife, Keturah, a dark-skinned woman and mother of several

Arabian/African tribes, etymologically may be linked with the Hebrew Ketoreth, 'frankincense,' suggestive in the words of one author, 'of South Arabian trade routes.' Of course, this depends on which came first, the name or the trade.)"[8]

"There were 797 hot and tired camels and donkeys"[9] in the Queen of Sheba's caravan, plus "mules and asses innumerable laden with gifts."[10] "They had labored 1,250 miles, carrying maximum loads of heavy gold and other jewelry, woods of numerous kinds, preserved foodstuffs, and hundreds of gallons of water picked up along the way. In the center of the caravan was the queen's veiled carriage made of weighty gold and hardwood. She was carried on the shoulders of young male servants."[11]

"Over 150 crack troops of the palace guard and the Ethiopian army march in the royal section with the Queen. Thirty or more handmaidens, cooks, beauticians and skilled craftsmen rode in either wagon-like vehicles or perched atop camels. The queen needed with her other craftsmen, such as jewelers, leather workers, map readers, chemists, priests, magicians, philosophers, astrologers, and other men who knew how to guide the ships of the desert. These 'ships' carried twenty million dollars worth of gifts. The man who knew how to guide caravans best was the skilled merchant and traveler, Tamrin. He traveled this route to Solomon's kingdom before. As a matter of fact, the King of Judah sent word to him 1,300 miles away. King Solomon had heard of Tamrin's reputation as an excellent salesman. He had wanted from Ethiopia some of the gold, emeralds, some fragrant woods, incense and other Ethiopian items which Tamrin sold to the known world."[12]

King Solomon watched her from afar as she came down the trail to Jerusalem. He was very interested in the Queen of

8   Woolsey, Raymond H. Men and Women of Color in the Bible, p. 52.
9   Hyman, Mark. Blacks Who Died for Jesus, p. 70.
10 Jones, A. H. M. and Monroe, Elizabeth. A History of Abyssinia, p. 11.
11 Hyman, Mark. Blacks Who Died for Jesus, p. 70.
12 Ibid., p. 70.

Sheba, because King Solomon was acquainted with black and dark-skinned people.

Bathsheba, his mother, was dark-skinned and her name means "daughter of Sheba." Sheba is one of the sons of Cush, which means "black" or "Ethiopian." Sheba was another ancient name for a black nation (Genesis 10:7). Her name also means "Bathshuz," which is a Canaanite name. It is a descriptive name of the inhabitants of the land of Sheba or Ethiopia. This name usually is descriptive of a person of dark skin.

Bathsheba was married to Uriah, the son of Heth, who is a descendant of Ham. The black race came from Ham, because the first son of Ham was Cush, which means "Ethiopia."

The Bible states very plainly that Uriah was a Hittite, so his wife, being of the same culture, probably was a Gentile also. We assume that Bathsheba, Uriah's wife, was of the same dark-skinned culture. Uriah, son of Heth (father of the Hittites), was the second son of Canaan (Genesis 10:5), the son of Ham, the father of the black race, who the Bible states had a beautiful wife (See 2 Samuel 12:10).

David became involved with Bathsheba while she was yet Uriah's wife; then he had Uriah killed so he could take Bathsheba as his own wife. The king had beautiful women all around him, but there was something special about this woman who took David's mind off the battle with the Philistines. All he could think about was Bathsheba. This drove him to a sinful relationship with her.

After God judged David's sin, he blessed David and Bathsheba with another son who was named Solomon.

We know that Solomon was aware of the Ethiopians, if not from the Law, from his own mother.

Philip had to go to the Ethiopian, because there was a destiny spoken of throughout the Scriptures in relation to these black people. They were united with the Jews in their journeys into the land of promise.

The Ethiopians had entered into covenant with God under the Law of Moses. The very land that God gave the Jews was the land of Canaan. Canaan was the son of Ham. This is where we get the name "Canaanite." Ham was the originator of the black race.

"As the vanguard approached the temple, the caravan was changed and the Queen of Sheba was brought to the head of the column."[13] When the nobles and king's advisors approached the Queen, she acknowledged each and in return presented her own nobles and top military. "Tamrin was saved for last, because he was her most valuable friend. He had told her about wise King Solomon and the marvelous kingdom of Judah."[14]

"The white cotton robe of purity told of her virginity. It was made from the product of the tree cotton from her country."[15]

Solomon made a statement in his greeting to Queen Makeda that, "It is known throughout the world that Judah and Ethiopia have been friends since any of us can remember, since the days of the Kenites."[16] They continued in their greetings and royal protocol. "Solomon entertained her honorably, giving her food in abundance and eleven changes of raiment every day."[17]

The Bible says:

> ...when she [the queen] was come to Solomon, she communed with him of all that was in her heart.
>
> And Solomon told her all questions: there was not any thing hid from the king, which he told her not.
>
> - 1 Kings 10:2,3

13   Ibid., p. 71.
14   Ibid., p. 71.
15   Ibid., p. 72.
16   Ibid., p. 74.
17   Jones, A.H. M. and Monroe, Elizabeth. A History of Abyssinia, p. 11.

That could cover a lot of ground, for we are told, "...he was wiser than all men..." (1 Kings 4:31). "He was conversant concerning botany and zoology; he spoke three thousand proverbs and composed fifteen hundred songs."[18]

"Makeda had access to an abundance of gold which she shared with King Solomon. In a few days Solomon had built a throne beside his own for Makeda."[19]

"She stayed many months marvelling at the wisdom with which Solomon directed the artificers and communing with him on matters of religion, and before long she abandoned the worship of the sun and the moon and the stars and worshipped the God of Israel."[20]

In "Ethiopia, A Cultural History" by Sylvia Pankhurst, "She is acclaimed of as a 'woman of splendid beauty' who introduced the religion and culture of Israel to her own land."[21]

"Makeda received most of Solomon's attention. However, at that moment, the king had 700 wives and 300 concubines. Among his wives were Nitocris, daughter of the king of Egypt; Sulamit, daughter of King Suman, a longtime friend; Rachel, daughter of Hiram II, king of Tyre; Terada, daughter of the king of Sidon; and Emmah, daughter of Achbal, king of far distant Ceyon. Yet he made Makeda his immediate and favorite queen."[22]

"The Jews at various periods in their history on minor and on major levels took wives from many foreign nations"[23] The Bible substantiates this:

> But king Solomon loved many strange women, together with the daughter of Pharaoh, women of the

18   Woolsey, Raymond H. Men and Women of Color in the Bible, p. 54.
19   Hyman, Mark. Blacks Who Died for Jesus, p. 75.
20   Jones, A. H. M. and Monroe, Elizabeth. A History of Abyssinia, p. 11.
21   Clark, John Henrick. "Africa in Early World History," Ebony Magazine, August, 1976, p. 127.
22   Hyman, Mark. Blacks Who Died for Jesus, p. 75.
23   Rhoades, F. S. Black Characters and References of the Holy Bible, p. 52.

> Moabites, Ammonites, Edomites, Zidonians, and Hittites.

> And he had seven hundred wives, princesses, and three hundred concubines: and his wives turned away his heart.

> - 1 Kings 11:1,3

"Thus, the black inhabitants of the nations as well as other foreign people became a part of the nation of Israel."[24] "The Kebra Nagast condones Solomon's many wives as a way to fulfill God's promise to Abraham, that his seed should be as the stars of heaven."[25]

"At length after six months Makeda resolved that she must return and look to her kingdom. When Solomon heard of her purpose he said in his heart, 'A woman of such splendid beauty has come to me from the ends of the earth. Will God give me seed in her?' It is speculated that Solomon's desire for seed in Makeda was not due to lust, but to the desire to raise up many sons who would inherit the cities of the world and destroy their idols."[26]

"Solomon determined to fulfill his purpose, and he invited the queen to a farewell feast and served her dishes full of pepper and vinegar such as would make her thirst. At the conclusion of the feast, since it had drawn late, he invited the queen to sleep in his palace. The queen hesitated, but at length consented if Solomon would swear not to take her by force, for she was a virgin. The king agreed, and demanded from her in return an oath that she would not take by force anything that was in his palace. To this she agreed without demur, protesting that she was not a thief. So two beds were spread on either side of the royal bedchamber, and they retired. The queen slept a little, but presently she awoke and her throat was parched.

24 Ibid., p. 52.
25 Woolsey, Raymond H. Men and Women of Color in the Bible, p. 54.
26 Jones, A. H. M. and Monroe, Elizabeth. A History of Abyssinia, p. 11.

Now the king had bidden his servants set a jar of water in the center of the room"[27]

"That night, thirsty from the spicy foods, she took a drink of water when she thought Solomon was asleep."[28] "But Solomon was not asleep. He leaped out of the bed, grabbed her arms and said: 'Thou hast broken the oath that thou hast sworn not to take anything by force that is in my palace.' The queen argued that the oath didn't apply to water, but the king replied that there was nothing on earth more precious than water. The queen admitted that she was wrong, but begged that she might drink. So Solomon was released from his oath and he worked his will on her, and they slept together."[29] Some say he "seduced her."[30]

"As King Solomon slept with the Queen of Sheba, Makeda, sometimes referred to in history as 'Bilkis,' her dynastic name,"[31] "the king dreamed a dream, and he saw that the sun came down to the land of Judah and illuminated it very brightly, and immediately it removed to Ethiopia and shone there. And a second time it came to the land of Judah, but the Jews hated it and strove to destroy it, and it departed to the lands of Rome and Ethiopia."[32]

The Kebra Nagast, purports that the Ethiopians believed they had been chosen by God to succeed the Jews, who had failed their divine mission.[33]

"Makeda was almost six months into her pregnancy when she finally decided to leave for Ethiopia. She was thoroughly converted to the Jewish religion and promised to take it to her

27   Ibid., p. 11.
28   Yeshag. Nebra Nagast, "Glory of the Kings."
29   Jones, A. H. M. and Monroe, Elizabeth. A History of Abyssinia, pp. 11,12.
30   Reader's Digest. Atlas of the Bible, p. 105.
31   Bent, Theodore. The Sacred City of the Ethiopians, p. 166.
32   Jones, A. H. M. and Monroe, Elizabeth. A History of Abyssinia, p. 12.
33   Woolsey, Raymond H. Men and Women of Color in the Bible, p. 51.

kingdom and her people. On leaving, Solomon gave her a ring. He said, 'If a son is born to you, give him this ring and send him here to me." [34]

Makeda went back to Ethiopia, because she had a kingdom to rule even though Solomon did not want her to return. She wanted her child to be born in her own homeland in order that he would have rights to the throne. [35]

The Queen of Sheba went back to Ethiopia during her last three months of pregnancy. It was a long journey. As she crossed the Ethiopian border, she went into labor and bore a son, who she named Ebna Hakim, which means "son of a wise man." [36]

34 Hyman, Mark. Blacks Who Died for Jesus, p. 75.
35 Ibid., p. 75.
36 Ibid., pp. 75,76.

Chapter 9

The Son born to Solomon and the Queen of Sheba

"Ebna Hakim, son of Queen Makeda of Sheba, had grown to manhood. He had grown up under firm royal teachings and at twenty-one he was a scholar, a warrior, a young man with a mind of his own. He knew the story of his birth, that twenty-one years earlier, his mother had traveled to the land of Judah. She had been converted by King Solomon to the Judean religion and had worshipped at the flow of knowledge from this wise king."[37]

"A great and inevitable influence of Ebna Hakim growing up was the constant reminder that he was indeed the son of the King of Judah. Yet, he learned more about his mother's people, a lineage which went back to 1370 B.C. There had been a split in the major political party. A man named ZaAngabo replaced the last representative of the elder dynasty of the Arwe royal line. It was ZaAngabo's family which ruled Ethiopia for 350 years. Ebna Hakim had heard much about ZaSebado, his great-grandfather and his great-grandmother, Ceres. He had been a precious grandchild to Queen Ismenie."[38]

"On his twenty-first birthday, Makeda gave Ebna Hakim the ring. It had taken him twenty-one years to grow into its

---

37   Ibid., p. 76.
38   Ibid., p. 76.

neat fitting."[39] He took the ring and went to visit his father, Solomon.

Tamrin, the merchant, went with Ebna Hakim, also called Menelik, to visit his father, Solomon. Queen Makeda sent Menelik with a great company of people under the charge of Tamrin, and she bade Tamrin to ask King Solomon to anoint Menelik king and make a law that from henceforth none but the male issue of Menelik should rule in Ethiopia—for up to that time queens had reigned in Ethiopia."[40]

"When Menelik arrived in Jerusalem he was mistaken for Solomon and messengers went to Solomon saying: 'Behold, one has come to our land who resembled thee in every feature.' And Solomon enquired from whence he had come and they said, 'We asked him not, for he seemed to be one of great authority, but his followers said they were of Ethiopia.' And King Solomon rejoiced in his heart, for though he had married many wives, God had confounded his purposes and he had but one son, Rehoboam, at this point."[41]

"As Solomon walked toward the tall, muscular young man, he gasped. He was the spitting image of King David, father of Solomon."[42] "He then summoned Menelik to come before him, and Menelik gave Solomon the ring, but Solomon said, 'What need is there of the ring? Without a sign I know thee that thou art my son.'"[43]

Even though the ring helped to officially identify Menelik to Solomon, it is said everyone in the palace could recognize the resemblance of the young visitor to their monarch. By this time, Solomon was old. He was also debauched through much wine and many women. Worst of all, he had largely abandoned the worship of the true God, whose religion Makeda had accepted and taught to Menelik. Solomon was now honoring

39 Ibid, p. 78.
40 Jones, A. H. M. and Monroe, Elizabeth. A History of Abyssinia, p. 12.
41 Ibid., p. 13.
42 Hyman, Mark. Blacks Who Died for Jesus, p. 78.
43 Jones, A. H. M. and Monroe, Elizabeth. A History of Abyssinia, p. 13.

Baal, Moloch, and the gods of Egypt (See 1 Kings 11:1-8). Menelik felt it his divinely ordained mission to rescue the true religion that he had actually grown up with. The God of Israel was at this point probably more important to Menelik than to his Jewish father, Solomon.[44]

"Banquets, joyous feasts, and spontaneous celebrations never ended in honor of Ebna Hakim."[45]

"Rehoboam, the second son of Solomon and the half-brother of Ebna Hakim, stood close by. He had helped escort the young African to the king. Rehoboam could interpret the exciting vibration coming from Solomon. He could feel that his proud father would step down for this African. He could feel the outpouring of love and the power of heritage which went naturally to the firstborn son."[46]

Some considered Rehoboam as Solomon's firstborn, labeling him this from the Jewish lineage, but the firstborn son of Solomon was Ebna Hakim. Firstborn sons bring much joy to their fathers. They are referred to as the beginning of the father's strength (See Genesis 49:3).

History tells us that Solomon was about to have a coronation to crown Ebna Hakim king of Israel because he was the firstborn son. However, Rehoboam, the second born, even though he was considered the firstborn on the Jewish side, immediately confronted Solomon, promising to lead a revolt against Israel if Solomon crowned Ebna Hakim as king.

Later, Rehoboam did lead a revolt, which is partially responsible for the split of Israel's twelve tribes.

The meaning of Solomon's name is "man of peace or restful." Dominated by this nature, Solomon backed off and did not make Ebna Hakim king.

---

44   Woolsey, Raymond H. <u>Men and Women of Color in the Bible</u>, p. 54.
45   Hyman, Mark. <u>Blacks Who Died for Jesus</u>, p. 78.
46   <u>Ibid.</u>, p. 78

Solomon made Rehoboam king of Israel and had a coronation to crown and anoint Ebna Hakim with holy oil as the king of Ethiopia.[47] "Then Solomon crowned Ebna Hakim king of Ethiopia."[48] He then sent him back as the king of Ethiopia to crown his mother the queen of Ethiopia, because she had only been queen of a section called "Sheba."[49]

Menelik (Ebna Hakim) did not intend to stay. He went intending to visit, and then return to the Queen of Sheba, his mother. Solomon wanted him to stay. History tells us that "Solomon tried to persuade Menelik to stay and reign in Israel for he was his firstborn son. But Menelik would not."[50]

When Solomon crowned Ebna Hakim as king of Ethiopia, Solomon sent a whole generation of the next leaders to be with Ebna Hakim in Ethiopia. All the oldest sons of the tribe of Judah, the praisers and rulers, were sent to Ethiopia. He added to this number the oldest sons of leading families. Twelve of them were judges. Solomon sent a total of 12,000 Israelites to take up permanent residence in Ethiopia with Ebna Hakim, a thousand of them being Levites. Today, Ethiopian Jews trace their lineage to these 12,000 Jews, because they intermingled and married one another. In fact, today the kings of Ethiopia claim to come from the lineage of Solomon.[51]

History states that "Solomon said to his counselors and officers: 'I am sending my firstborn son to rule in Ethiopia. Do ye also and send your firstborn sons to be his counselors and officers.' And they obeyed the king's command."[52]

Solomon also sent the son of Zadok, Azariah (1 Kings 4:2), meaning "one who protects or one who surrounds." It is the same name given for "helpmeet." Solomon sent Azariah to be

47 Jones, A. H. M. and Monroe, Elizabeth. A History of Abyssinia, p. 13.
48 Hyman, Mark. Blacks Who Died for Jesus, p. 79.
49 Ibid., p. 79.
50 Jones, A. H. M. and Monroe, Elizabeth. A History of Abyssinia, p. 13.
51 Hyman, Mark. Blacks Who Died for Jesus, p. 79.
52 Jones, A. H. M. and Monroe, Elizabeth. A History of Abyssinia, p. 13.

the priest with the 1,000 Levites to cause the religion of the Jews to flourish in Ethiopia.[53]

Solomon attempted to give them a plan that would not fail in assuring that the Law and the God of Israel would become the God of Ethiopia also. A copy of the Law of the Covenant was also given to Ebna Hakim, his son.[54] "And Zadok, the high priest, expounded to Ebna Hakim the law of Israel and pronounced upon him blessings if he should keep it and curses if he should leave it."[55]

Solomon had a model of the ark of the covenant to be taken to Ethiopia, because the Levites were to serve as priests before it. God was not against it, because the Ethiopians had been in league with the Jews and the promise was, "Whatever good comes to us goes to you."

Remember, Moses was married to an Ethiopian woman, and it is quite certain that her family members were with her. Jethro was there all the time, and Zipporah's sisters were there. Jethro helped set up the government, so when God gave the law and the covenant, an Ethiopian remnant was also there. The Ethiopian remnant took the presence of the Lord with them.

"When Menelik had departed, Solomon was sad at heart, and he told Zadok of the dream that he had dreamed the night he lay with the Queen of Ethiopia. And Zadok was smitten with fear and said: 'Would that you had told me of this dream before, for I fear that Our Lady of Zion is departed.' And he went into the sanctuary and took off the two under coverings and beheld the model of the Ark which Azariah his son had caused to be made because of the 'sorrow of the firstborn sons of the nobles and counselors of Israel at leaving their native land.'"[56] "And Zadok wept and beat his breast and fell in a stupor. Soon someone came and saw Zadok and went and told

---

53   Hyman, Mark. Blacks Who Died for Jesus, p. 79.
54   Ibid., p. 79.
55   Jones, A. H. M. and Monroe, Elizabeth. A History of Abyssinia, p. 13.
56   Ibid., p. 14.

Solomon what was wrong. And Solomon arose with his host and pursued after the Ethiopians. And after many days, Solomon despaired of pursuing them and lamented greatly. But the spirit of prophecy comforted him saying: 'Our lady of Zion has not been given to an alien but to thine own firstborn son.'"[57]

History declares that God said it was all right, because His Ark would rest in Ethiopia with His people and Solomon's firstborn. The glory was to depart and to be preserved in Ethiopia.[58] And Solomon was comforted and returned to Jerusalem. Upon his return, he charged all his counselors and officers to keep secret the loss of the Ark of the Covenant, and so the children of Israel knew not that it had departed.[59]

Ebna Hakim went back and crowned Makeda the queen of all of Ethiopia. She died some 35-40 years later, about 955 B.C. Ebna Hakim then came to full power and changed his name to Menelik.[60]

History later records, "Now Balthazar, king of Rome, had no son but only three daughters. And he sent to King Solomon and asked that he would send one of his sons to marry one of his daughters and rule over the kingdom of Rome. And Solomon sent Adramis, his youngest son, and with him the youngest sons of his counselors and officers. And Rehoboam ruled over Judah, and Menelik ruled over all the lands to the south and east, and Adramis ruled over all the lands to the north and west. And so was fulfilled the prophecy that the seed of David and Solomon should rule over all the world."[61]

"The Ethiopian Constitution, promulgated under Emperor Haile Selassie, averred that the king was descended 'without interruption from the dynasty of Menelik I, son of the Queen of Ethiopia, the Queen of Sheba, and King Solomon of Jerusalem.' The Kebra Nagast purports to carry the lineage

57 Ibid., p. 15.
58 Ibid., p. 14.
59 Ibid., p. 15.
60 Hyman, Mark. Blacks Who Died for Jesus, p. 80.
61 Jones, A. H. M. and Monroe, Elizabeth. A History of Abyssinia, p. 15.

back to Moses. However, Solomon was of the tribe of Judah, whereas Moses was a Levite."[62] Perhaps the lineage back to Moses is on the Queen of Sheba's side through Moses' Ethiopian wife, Zipporah (See Numbers 12:1). This would be highly feasible since for several dynasties, Ethiopia or Sheba was ruled by queens, thereby making the women's lineage important under that culture.

The Ethiopians, through their relationship with Solomon and his firstborn son, Menelik, had the "Ark of His Glory" or a copy, and Azariah, the priest, along with 1,000 Levites, to serve before this Ark in the land of Sheba.

It seems strange that we do not hear anything in the Bible about the Ark after this time period and after Solomon's reign. It also seems strange that the nation of Israel lost power as a nation after Solomon's reign and the split of the ten tribes (See 1 Kings 12). Israel never came to power or prominence again.

Later in Israel's history, King Hezekiah brought a reformation to Judah and did that which was right in the sight of God, as did David, his father (See 2 Chronicles 29). He re-established the brazen altar and the burnt offering as a part of Israel's ordinance to worship. But the Scripture never says they re-established the Ark of the Covenant to the temple during this restoration of worship in Israel. They cleansed the temple, they found the Law, but the Scripture does not say anything about them finding the Ark in the temple.

Scripture says that they went into the temple and relit the Candlestick; they repaired the gates; they cleansed the filthiness out of the holy place and started the burnt offering. When the burnt offering was started again, the song of the Lord also started again and they offered more sacrifices. Their worship remained before the brazen altar in the outer court, but no mention is made of the Ark of the Covenant. It is never mentioned again as being in the holy place of worship after Solomon's reign. The same is true for the reformation and

---

62 Woolsey, Raymond H. <u>Men and Women of Color in the Bible</u>, p. 51.

restoration of worship during the reign of King Joash (See 2 Chronicles 24), and also during the reign of King Josiah (See 2 Chronicles 34).

My conclusion for this "lack of mention" of the Ark in Scripture is because the Ark was taken to Ethiopia with Solomon's firstborn son, Menelik (Ebna Hakim).

Why did Solomon do this? Because the Ethiopians had a destiny with Israel and they had a covenant. The Gospel went to the Ethiopian eunuch, Endich, not out of coincidence, but out of <u>covenant</u>. Because there was a covenant, "Whatever good God gave to Israel was to go to the Ethiopians, too." Solomon wanted their kingdom to be governed by the Law and rule of Jehovah God, the God of Israel.

There is a destiny all the way through the Bible for the black culture, and it is for us to find it out and come under God's righteousness; then answer the call of destiny which has been upon our lives for a long time.

In July, 1986, thousands of Ethiopian Jews were airlifted from their country to Israel. Israel went to Ethiopia by way of Sudan and airlifted the Jewish Ethiopians and brought them back to their homeland to enjoy a better life. In other words, Israel went down and freed the Ethiopians from the bondage of famine, pestilence, and disease and brought them to their own homeland. They did this based on two covenants: Moses' covenant with the Ethiopians, calling it "Operation Moses," and Solomon's covenant with the queen of Sheba and his son, calling it "Operation Sheba."[63]

We need to see the spiritual parallel in the Body of Christ. At the present time, the greater Israel, the Church, is freeing spiritual Ethiopia to enjoy life in the promises of God and in the land of God. It is time to recognize that God has given destiny to the black segment of the Church in His Word.

---

63 Safran, Claire. "Secret Exodus: The Story of Operation Moses from a Forthcoming Book," <u>Reader's Digest</u>, January, 1987, pp. 96-104;179-206.

It is time to get this Gospel out of storytelling and out of emotional release, and bring it to where it is relevant to everyday life. Jesus always made the Gospel relevant to where the people lived. Now, the Gospel of the Kingdom is coming to the black segment of the Body of Christ to lift us up from spiritual poverty, spiritual disease, and spiritual famine to the place where we belong in the purposes and plans of God.

Let the shackles of deprivation fall off you now, and rise up to the call of destiny that is upon your life. The Church of Jesus Christ awaits the black segment of the Body of Christ to bring a fresh revelation of Jesus Christ to the Church world that will bring solutions to the many problems that they face.

Let us answer the call to be "eyes in the wilderness" to "keep the Church of Jesus Christ in the way."

Chapter 10

We Cannot Export Racism

And this gospel of the kingdom shall be preached in all the world for a witness unto all nations; and then shall the end come.

- Matthew 24:14

This verse is a key Scripture now for the Church in the United States, because God is admonishing the Church to be concerned for the nations. This is the cry of the Holy Spirit all over the United States. This concern is being voiced by many major leaders who feel the burden to reach the nations. However, with this concern, God said to me, "This is My burden, but I rebuke you, America. You are not going to reach the nations of what is called the Third World until you reach your own nation." The word <u>nation</u> means "race."

Until the Church in America can reach the race that is closest to them and bring a Kingdom witness and lifestyle of the Gospel to them, then God is not going to use them to affect other nations in a lasting and eternal way.

I attended a meeting in Dallas in 1986 at which the Holy Spirit spoke: **"If you are going to take the Gospel to every nation, you cannot export racism. I will not allow the Church to export racism. You are going to have to get things together in the Church in America."**

God is dealing with race relations in the Church so we can affect the nations. Ninety percent of the world is non-white. Only ten percent of the world is white, yet most whites control the world. For the Church in America to reach out to the nations, they must reach out to the people of the black culture and to other dark-skinned ethnic groups.

It becomes a responsibility to those who have embraced some measure of the Kingdom to bring that witness, first of all, to the nation (or race) closest to them, or in a sense, to the nations with whom they have the most trouble. The early church experienced persecution before they would obey God. They didn't willingly take the Gospel to the world. They didn't want to leave the area of Jerusalem, nor had they settled within themselves that it was time to take the Gospel of the Kingdom to every nation (race).

In the book of Jeremiah, God took His own people into captivity, not to destroy them, but to deliver them from the idol gods they served.

The Gospel will no longer be bound by our bondages.

Even though God will not violate our will, He has a lot of ways to make us willing. He knows how to make us willing. God had to bring pressure to the Jews to drive them to obedience. Tribulation works patience. Pressure works patience. The word <u>patience</u> means "to keep you under." Patience is hopeful and cheerful endurance.

The Church in America has not been obedient to the Commission of God. The early church was not immediately obedient to the call of God to take this Gospel into all the world, so God allowed tribulation to work them back under the Commission. They were satisfied in Jerusalem, so God allowed some persecution to drive them to other cultures (nations).

Church and Society's Confrontation with Racism

Contrary to popular teaching that Cornelius was the first non-Jew to receive the Gospel, Endich, the Ethiopian enuch, was the first convert after the half-Jewish Samaritans.

Just as the worth of black people as a whole has been trampled under foot in America, there has also been an attempt to hide the value of the black race in the Bible. Blacks have done a lot of things that have added to the fulfillment of God's purposes in Biblical history as well as in American history.

Though Satan has tried to obscure a God-given purpose and destiny to black people, God is bringing renewed understanding concerning His desire to use Spiritual Ethiopia to fulfill His will in these last days.

Much of the economic progress of America was gained on the burdened backs of black slaves. There seems to be a perpetual desire of Satan to keep blacks bent over under the weight of oppression and sin, even as Simon, the black Cyrenian, helped bear the burden of Jesus' cross. The Lord once spoke to my heart and said, "Don't ever forget that in My most trying time, a black man came out of the shadows and helped Me bear My cross."

Many white racist organizations have met in churches to strategize a means of continuous hate and aggression. The Church in general has failed to be a voice and vehicle of conviction against this type of hate. One of the Church's problems in the 1960's was that they failed to receive Dr. Martin Luther King, Jr., as a prophet to the nation who was sent to make America aware of the injustices of society that were done to black Americans. The Church had the opportunity during that time to join Dr. King and others in ending Civil War and beginning the process of really laying the axe of God's Word and His Spirit to the roots of hate, racism, and bigotry. Since the Church did not respond, the movement spearheaded by Dr. King became political, and the axe was never laid to the spiritual roots of hate, racism, and bigotry.

As the Holy Spirit brings visitations to the black segment of the Body of Christ (Spiritual Ethiopia) and imparts purpose, ministry, and solutions to this segment that will eventually help solve some of the problems that affect the entire Church, my prayer is that the Church world will receive black Christians. I believe this is the key to helping the Church achieve the greatness that is ordained for Christendom in this hour.

I am not talking about tokenism, tolerance, or integration. I am talking about the new creation...the new creation where there is neither Jew nor Greek (no racial distinctions); neither bond nor free (no class distinctions); neither Barbarian nor Scythian (no cultural distinctions); neither male nor female (no sexual distinctions); but Christ is all and in all, and we are one in Him (See Galatians 3:28 and Colossians 3:11).

My prayer is that we not miss the visitation of God in reconciling the races in the Church and that we become one - that the world will finally recognize that the Father has sent Jesus Christ as the Lord and Savior of the world.

Chapter 11

My Personal Deliverance from Racism

God who knows all things knew I was a radical. He knew my background, and He knew I was a strong racist. From the time I was a child, I could identify right and wrong. I saw all the wrong things that were done to black people, and I was not one to keep my mouth shut and be quiet about wrong.

In fact, I could not stand wrong, even if it was not affecting me. I would speak up for someone else. If a teacher explained something that I knew was wrong, I would say, "That's not right." The teacher would say, "Hush, Mr. Edwards." Then I'd end up in the office of the principal, who sometimes would simply suspend me for a period of time, instead of dealing with the wrong. I was bad, but not for bad's sake. I saw things that were wrong and tried to right the wrongs in my own way.

God used me in the evangelistic field before I began to pastor. I didn't like pastoring, I didn't like pastors, and I didn't want anything to do with them, but I loved going out on the evangelistic field.

God used me in demonstration of the power of the Spirit as a young man. I have seen the miraculous continuously from the beginning of ministry.

I know the power of God, and I know why God for His own reasons cuts off the power so we will not be destroyed.

Most of my beginning ministerial experience was in white circles. I was pursued by an organization that patronizes testimonies and didn't care too much about a person's character.

Their main concern was that you had a gift which would draw a crowd.

I am often used in the word of knowledge and in healing and, of course, that draws crowds. An ability to identify infirmities supernaturally and pronounce them healed drew the crowds.

I have kept a list of people who were healed in my meetings and who are still healed today. I have been in churches where I pointed to one side of the church building and the entire congregation fell backward. I didn't push them! I simply pointed at them. God let me touch those dimensions.

Then God spoke to me. "Do you want to go on with Me?" I thought He was going to announce, "Move over, Billy Graham, here comes Jeff Edwards."

God said to me, "Jeff, you know the calling on your life. You know the anointing is there. You know I have gifted you. Now, I want you to go and submit all you have to this particular church."

I said, "Well, fine. Thank You, Lord." He said, "I want to process you. I want to deal with your character. If you continue on in the way you are going, you will be destroyed. I must back you off and deal with you."

I was obedient and went to Evangelistic Center Church in Kansas City, only to find that it was 90 percent white.

God was dealing with me, and He was processing me by sending me to the thing I opposed the most. God was taking me from my culture and race by sending me to a white church in order to establish me. This was the beginning of God's extensive dealing in my life. They didn't have to preach one word in that church. I was dealt with by just sitting in the congregation. Me, militant Jeff Edwards, had to sit in this church filled with white folks.

I kept asking myself, "What am I going to learn from some white folks?" I was ticked at God! I was looking for anything, just the misquoting of a Scripture, and I purposed that I would leave that place. When I first attended this church, I did not accept the pastor of the church as my spiritual father. It was perhaps good that he was out of town when I first arrived at his church, because the person who drew me did so with pure love. This was the late Sister Margaret Rowden. She glowed! (I found out later that the glow was from the life, light, and love of God within her.)

When I first went to that church, I was full of hate and disgust. Even though I was saved, that hate was not gone, and it didn't disappear overnight. My hate had roots that went deep in my soul and spirit.

When I first went to Evangelistic Center Church, a white-headed lady in a bright yellow dress came up to me who said, "Hello, brother." She hugged me. I had never experienced such pure love in all my life. It unsettled me. I went home and said, "What does that woman want?" I had dreams about that woman. She messed up my whole life and all she said was, "Hello, brother" and hugged me...but the pure love of God in her started breaking down all the racism that was within me. God sent me to the thing I opposed the most in order to deal with me.

Sometimes God will confront you with the thing that you fear or hate the most. If you can't face things you fear the most, you are not ready for God's dealings, for God will cause you to confront the thing you dislike or fear the most so you can be purified and cleansed.

I didn't become involved in this church for a while. I sat on the outside of the activities as a non-participant. It is easy to sit in a church and never get into the core of the church. I never got into the heartbeat of the church. I was, however, enjoying this church while I remained involved in a denominational church.

I would almost crawl up the steps of this church hungering for the truth, because I was so beat down from the traditional church's rejection of the vision and ministry to which God had called me. If an interpretation of tongues was not right, I never knew it. Everything blessed me. I was just waiting for the song of the Lord to be sung. Everything in the service seemed to talk to me.

Someone would turn to me and say, "Praise the Lord. God is dealing with us." I would answer, "Praise God." Then I would write that down. That was for me. God was dealing with me, and He did a quick work.

At the same time, some people in that church admitted that they were delivered from a lot of prejudice because of my attitude. They said they were delivered from strong hatred and prejudice when I said, "Hello" to them in the love of God. Many of them said it was seeing me move in God, seeing my freedom in the Spirit, that God used to break down the walls and images that they had about black people.

God had to send me through the thing I opposed the most to break some things in me. This became a great humbling process, a real tribulation workshop that was often very painful.

At this particular church, the real test came when an act of prejudice was publicly expressed. A word came to me out of a wrong spirit of prejudice, and it almost split me in half. All kinds of incidents happened, some which comforted me, some enhancing my anger and disappointment.

That old radical attitude of my past wanted to rise up and say, "All white folks are the same. They try to control and hinder the progress of black people. I tried to get along with you, and you tried to ruin me." That kind of rationale was in me, because of my background.

In spite of some of the things which happened, I knew I could not withdraw from that house of the Lord until God released me. I continued to attend and praised God, even though I was deeply hurt and would cry continuously. There was some prejudice toward me in this church, but I knew <u>how</u> I responded to the prejudice would be a key to my release into ministry.

I could have become bitter, but I chose to become better! The thing that was the most trying could have destroyed me if

I had taken it the wrong way. However, it advanced me. The thing that hurt me so bad and how I handled it was the very thing that, in God's time, released me into ministry. Hallelujah!

Within a year's time of this situation, I was ordained and sent out to fulfill the ministry that the Lord had entrusted to my care. I have learned that my reaction to racism and prejudice has a lot to do with my ability to help someone who is bound by this spirit. If I don't have a problem, I can help them solve their problem. I have learned that peace is not only action, but the absence of reaction!

Chapter 12

Prophetic Challenge to Spiritual Ethiopia

The physical airlift of Ethiopian Jews into the land of Israel, foreshadows a spiritual airlift taking place, putting the black segment of the Body of Christ into God-appointed positions of destiny.

Just as God used Jethro (a black priest and father-in-law of Moses) to train and help Moses, it is my belief that God is going to use the black segment of the Body of Christ to help the Church rise to her real call in these last days, especially in the areas of prayer, praise, worship, spiritual warfare, and the prophetic voice to the Church.

We know what happened to Moses. He had a divine encounter with God, who gave him a divine commission. Let's look at it in Exodus 3:1-4.

> *Now Moses kept the flock of Jethro his father in law, the priest of Midian: and he led the flock to the backside of the desert, and came to the mountain of God, even to Horeb.*
>
> *And the angel of the Lord [here's the divine encounter] appeared unto him in a flame of fire out of the midst of a bush: and he looked, and, behold, the bush burned with fire, and the bush was not consumed.*
>
> *And Moses said, I will now turn aside, and see this great sight, why the bush is not burnt.*

And when the Lord saw that he turned aside to see, God called unto him out of the midst of the bush, and said, Moses, Moses. And he said, Here am I.

God told Moses He was sending him to deliver the Israelites out of the hand of the Egyptians (Exodus 3).

Moses made all kinds of excuses why he wasn't qualified to deliver the Israelites.

...O my Lord, I am not eloquent, neither heretofore, nor since thou hast spoken unto thy servant: but I am slow of speech, and of a slow tongue.

And the Lord said unto him, Who hath made man's mouth? or who maketh the dumb, or deaf, or the seeing, or the blind? have not I the Lord?

Now therefore go, and I will be with thy mouth, and teach thee what thou shalt say.

- Exodus 4:10-12

Though Moses argued with God about his inability to deliver the Israelites, he obeyed the divine call.

Moses knew God had given Jethro to him as a father...one who would teach him how to shepherd, because he was going to shepherd millions of people.

Jethro [Moses' father-in-law and a black Ethiopian priest] trained Moses after he received his call.

Black Ethiopia and Black Egypt - A Covering, Atonement, and Reconciliation to Israel

And he said unto him, I will not go; but I will depart to mine own land, and to my kindred.

And he said, Leave us not, I pray thee; forasmuch as thou knowest how we are to encamp in the wilderness, and thou mayest be to us instead of eyes.

- Numbers 10:30,31

These verses show what the black Ethiopians were to be to the Israelites: EYES IN THE WILDERNESS. Their culture, nature, and background brought them a sight in the wilderness that the Israelites did not have. This was a natural sight that natural Ethiopia had, which I believe to be a parallel with the spiritual sight of spiritual Ethiopia.

Isaiah 43:3 says, **"For I AM the Lord thy God, the Holy One of Israel, thy Savior: I gave Egypt for thy ransom, Ethiopia and Seba for thee."**

The word ransom in Hebrew is *kopher.* It means a cover; that is, a village, as a covering. Specifically, it means bitumen (as used for coating) and the henna plant (as used for dyeing). Figuratively, it means "a redemption price." Some of the English translations for this word are "bribe, satisfaction, and sum of money."

The word *kopher* is a derivative of the word *kaphar,* which means to cover, specifically with bitumen. Figuratively, it means "to expiate or condone; to placate or cancel." Some English transliterations are "appease, make an atonement, cleanse, disannul, forgive, be merciful, pacify, pardon, purge away, put off, and to make reconciliation."

From this meaning, we can see that the black Ethiopians were as a covering for Israel in the wilderness. They were a traveling village as a covering from the inhabitants of the land, because the Ethiopians traveled in the wilderness and in the desert. They knew the land, and they were feared and respected by the other inhabitants of the land.

The black Ethiopians were like a blood covering, an atonement, a price of redemption, a bribe against all of the inhabitants of the land to protect the Israelites. They brought reconciliation (which means to bring to friendly terms) to the other nations in Israel's behalf.

These Ethiopians encountered the danger of the land before the Israelites ever came in contact with it. They had an inherent warlike nature which God used to strike fear in the inhabitants of the land. In the natural, they brought a respect to the Israelites that they didn't otherwise have.

Even the black nation of Egypt was a covering for Israel for a season when Pharaoh showed favor toward Joseph.

The warlike nature of the Ethiopians, inherent in many black people today, is a great asset if it is turned, not against people, but <u>against the demonic spirits</u> that have operated through people to oppress the black race and to keep this culture in a position of defeat. If that warlike nature is submitted to the cross, the Lord can resurrect it for His purposes.

There is a God-given destiny throughout the Scriptures in relation to His choosing the Jews as well as the Ethiopians. This is one of the reasons why I believe Satan has worked overtime to destroy the black race.

For example, we are losing our young black male children. The medical profession cannot give a reason why black male children die in the first 28 days of life more than any other species of children. Black male children, even after this period, are still in danger of dying in the first year of their lives. At the other end of the spectrum, many black men do not live a long time because of disease, high blood pressure, cancer, heart attacks, crime and being shot.

If the devil can wipe out the men, then he destroys a generation. In America, the blacks are like a time clock in what eventually happens to white America. Whatever happens in the black neighborhood (an oppressed segment of society) eventually will happen to the white segment of society. Statistics, however, always appear higher in an oppressed segment of society. For instance, unemployment in the black neighborhood is usually twice that of the national average.

The enemy wants to wipe out the black segment of society because of their God-given destiny, just as he has tried to wipe out the Jews. But here's the good news! Because the Jews had a sense of destiny as God's chosen people (though they didn't receive their Messiah), they could not be defeated by the enemy.

A lack of destiny among the black race has brought them very close to succumbing to the tactics of the devil.

God's Word says, "...**Whatsoever ye shall bind on earth shall be bound in heaven: and whatsoever ye shall loose on earth shall be loosed in heaven**" (Matthew 18:18).

As we learn to believe and speak God's Word above circumstances, God will lift the black segment of society from Satan's image of second-class citizenship into the image of Jesus Christ, for it is His desire that, no matter what our color, "...**we shall be like Him...**" (1 John 3:2).

Overcoming

The only hope of the Jews in this life has been a divine covenant. Their return in 1948 to their homeland after having no homeland for a while, was the fulfillment of a covenant. God said, "I will gather them." They are a part of destiny. God has brought the Jewish Ethiopians to their homeland, freeing them in the natural, and now they enjoy a land of promise that has always been theirs. God is also going to free spiritual Ethiopia (the black segment of the church) to their land of promise. <u>Now is God's hour in the lives of spiritual Ethiopians!</u>

Jesus said, "**And I, if I be lifted up from the earth, will draw <u>all men</u> unto me**" (John 12:32).

As black Christians lift up Jesus, they, too, are being moved into their destiny in Christ.

Just as the Ethiopians added to the Jewish culture, spiritual Ethiopians (black Christians) are an asset to the Body of Christ today. No longer are we a minus. In Christ, we are a **plus** to His plans and purposes. I believe that we will continue our destiny as warriors and <u>in Christ</u> conquer some areas in spiritual warfare that the church has been afraid to conquer.

The majority of the black segment of the church in America has never been able to get into position to receive the promises of God in a consistent manifestation. It seems as though black Christians have been like Simon of Cyrene who helped Jesus carry the cross. It's as if the devil has said, "You helped Jesus carry the cross, and I'm going to keep you blacks under the cross for the rest of your lives."

What I'm saying is that too many black Christians are still singing the blues, experiencing little of the victory that is available now in the Lord Jesus Christ. Because of this, they know little about the Kingdom of God, the will of God, and the government of God operating in their lives.

Through a slow progression, black Christians are moving over into the resurrection side of the Bible. Hallelujah! They are beginning to realize that in Christ Jesus they have a God-ordained destiny.

The blacks as a whole have been a "longsuffering" people. We have been an oppressed people, similar to the Jews under Egyptian bondage. We have been processed to be God's chosen people. I believe God will use blacks to bring the Church to her knees and to a place of purity.

I believe God's Word of the hour to the black segment of society is, "...who knoweth whether thou art come to the kingdom for such a time as this?" (Esther 4:14).

God wants the blacks and whites reconciled; that means to make things right before God, to bring us to righteousness (right standing before God and in right standing with one another).

For this to happen, we blacks must first be reconciled to one another in our own race. We must let forgiveness flow like a river over the spiritual raping, robbing, and stripping which we have long experienced and then believe God's Word in Isaiah 43:18 and 19.

> Remember ye not the former things, neither consider the things of old.
>
> Behold, I will do a new thing; now it shall spring forth; shall ye not know it? I will even make a way in the wilderness, and rivers in the desert.

As blacks and as whites, we are called to repentance and to righteousness. "...**Repent: for the kingdom of God is at hand**" (Matthew 4:17).

The black segment of the Body of Christ cannot belittle the call to repentance and the call to righteousness. Black Christians must get things right - come into right standing in Christ first and then with one another. Only then will we be in right standing with God to <u>every</u> race.

Reconciliation of blacks to blacks must begin in the church. This coming together in right relationship among the blacks is a prerequisite to the reconciliation that must then take place between the white and black races. Until reconciliation happens among ourselves, we will never answer the call of God of reconciliation to the white race.

Only as we begin to come together in Christ's love and for His purposes will the barriers between races begin to come down, allowing God to turn up the thermostat of His glory.

There must be a sense of purpose in black Christians in order to answer God's call of destiny to us as it relates to reconciliation in the church world. Where sin abounds, God's grace abounds in greater measure. God wants to give the black race His abundant grace to overcome anything negative that would attempt to hinder us from answering His call upon our lives.

Traditions in the black culture which have been satanically inspired must be dissolved. We must allow the Holy Spirit to bring truth to every facet of life, because all of God's works are done in truth (See Psalm 33:4), and He desires truth in the inward parts (See Psalm 51:6).

We must get right with God. We must come to a place of total consecration to the plans and purposes of God. We have to be willing (regardless of color of skin) to allow God to reach down into our lives and tear the works of hell out of us. Hell cannot reach the call of God. Hell has to be put down and heaven must rise up to deal with all of the inadequacies, sins, and habits in our lives. God has to deal with all of the cultural things that are contrary to His Kingdom so we can answer His call to reconciliation!

Chapter 13

Righteousness Exalts a Nation

God has been hindered from righting the wrongs of our society, because He has not had a people who have maintained a righteous standard. Even the white segment of the Church that has embraced the Kingdom of God has a righteousness toward God, but not necessarily toward one another.

Righteousness exalts a nation (See Proverbs 14:34). Righteousness exalts a race! Judge us right where we live, O Lord. Don't leave us in judgment, but bring us into righteousness.

"He shall judge thy people with righteousness, and thy poor with judgment" (Psalm 72:2). God cannot deal with unrighteousness until He has a righteous people. God has to have a people who will answer the call of righteousness in order to use those people to judge unrighteousness. He is establishing **trees** of righteousness, not flimsy leaves of righteousness which will dry up.

We have all experienced righteousness for a season, but someone crosses us the wrong way and pulls us right out of the love and righteousness of God. A tree of righteousness is a consistent standard of righteousness.

God wants you to deal with your latent lust; deal with your sin. He wants the roots of it removed. He wants you to experience total deliverance. He wants to right the wrongs of the poor, but He cannot touch the denominations if He doesn't have a people who will become a standard of righteousness.

"...the Lord God will cause righteousness and praise to spring forth before all the nations" (Isaiah 61:11).

Black Christians are to be a testimony in their lives, in their facilities, in their love one to another, in their homes, and in the raising of their children. Everything has to be a testimony of the Kingdom of God so that He can set a standard to others of what He has done in a people.

Because black Christians have not consistently maintained righteousness, they haven't freed God to deal with the inadequacies and discrepancies in society.

God is a God of equity, but He cannot right the wrongs if black Christians don't embrace His righteousness or come into right standing with Him. Many blacks did not believe God to change situations during the Civil Rights Movement. They did not believe God to right the wrongs.

The only way many blacks thought they could right the wrongs was to march and do something in their own efforts. They went out marching, but all they did was pray, "O God, we pray that You be with us, and don't let us get killed in Jesus' name. Amen." Personally, I am not against social action, but the roots of racism and prejudice cannot be dealt with through social action alone. The roots of racism and prejudice have not yet been dealt with. Only the Lord Jesus Christ and His Church can bring a spiritual reconciliation by laying the axe to the roots.

When a personal relationship with God is established and the entire Word of God is believed and acted upon, a racist, prejudiced, and oppressed society can be changed.

When true righteousness is presented, when true righteousness is accepted on both the horizontal and the vertical planes, when God can get a people established in righteousness, when righteousness and praise are before the nations, then He will make salvation come forth like burning. God will make salvation come forth like a lamp that burns. He will make your righteousness come like brightness. He will right the wrongs if He can get you right.

If my people, which are called by my name, shall humble themselves, and pray, and seek my face, and turn from their wicked ways; then will I hear from heaven, and will forgive their sin, and will heal their land.

- 2 Chronicles 7:14

Many blacks have not trusted in a God who can right wrongs, because they have not truly known the God of righteousness. Righteousness will not stop in the Church, but it will bleed out into the nations. God will right the wrongs if He can get us right.

That's why after Dr. Martin Luther King had a vision of the mountain, he said, "I've seen it. I've been to the mountain." The mountain he had been to was the mountain of the Kingdom of God! That's the only mountain worth mentioning. His comment was, "I've seen blacks and whites and Jews and Gentiles with hands joined together." Dr. King said, "I may not be there with you, but it is going to happen." He knew that all the things he had seen had to happen in the Church, because God only moves when **"My people will turn from their wicked ways."**

Does that mean God's people can have wicked ways? Yes! God's people, His saints, can have wicked ways. When we know things that we should do right and don't do them, it is wickedness. **"Therefore to him that knoweth to do good, and doeth it not, to him it is sin"** (James 4:17).

That goes from paying tithes to extending mercy. We've been taught what is right, but we don't always do what is right.

No matter what the situation, though, we are to forgive. Many times we hold grudges. We should come to church, but we neglect the assembling of ourselves together. We should love one another, but we pick and choose who we are going to love. To know what is right and not do it is wickedness. We should cry out, "Lord, deliver us from our wickedness."

If you receive God's judgments to get right, then He can judge the people with righteousness. He can right the wrongs.

He can right society. He can take men down, and He can elevate them. He can put down satanic factions. He can put down satanic oppressors. He can deal with men's affairs. He can remove man or change him."

> *When a man's ways please the Lord, he maketh even his enemies to be at peace with him.*

- Proverbs 16:7

Righteousness Promotes Peace

When we resist God's righteousness, we end up in tumult and unrest and are unable to abide in peace. The peace of God comes by righteousness.

> *But the wisdom that is from above is first pure, then peaceable, gentle, easy to be intreated, full of mercy and good fruits, without partiality, and without hypocrisy.*
>
> *And the fruit of righteousness is sown in peace of them that make peace.*

- James 3:17,18

God's peace comes to us by His righteousness or right wisdom being established and embraced.

> *He shall judge thy people with righteousness, and thy poor with judgment.*
>
> *The mountains shall bring peace to the people, and the little hills, by righteousness.*

- Psalm 72:2,3

The mountain speaks of the house of the Lord, the Kingdom of God, and the Kingdom of God is righteousness and peace in the Holy Ghost. When I receive righteousness, I can receive peace, which means "to be in harmony, to be at one, and to be in union with God." As soon as I get the foundation laid right and as soon as righteousness is established, I can follow through with peace. As a people, we need to come to peace, and we need it first inside of ourselves.

Many black people are disturbed inside and worry about things they should not worry about. When there is so much turmoil inside, we are not able to reach out and help others.

One half of our families have no male figure (70 percent in large urban cities). Most of our mothers are raising children alone. We have a need to come to peace with God so that we can come to peace with one another. There is no need to talk about drawing the line and bringing unity with whites when we cannot bring unity among ourselves. If we are warring on the inside, we will be warlike toward each other. Only the person of peace can fight effectively in God's war.

Let's explore something about the Ethiopians. In the natural, they were warlike people and quick to fight. They would move in league with anyone to fight, but they chose the wrong league when they came against Israel and God whipped their socks off (See 2 Chronicles 14). That part of the black culture must go! We had to be warlike to survive, but we have become victims of our own oppression. In the oppression and the process of survival, we forgot who to trust. Blacks don't even trust one another. Everyone talks about racism, but most black people will follow a white person quicker than they will follow each other.

We must come to a right relationship with God and right relationship with each other if we are to be at peace with God and with one another.

The first thing the mountain of God's house will do is send us real peace. We cannot give peace to people who are not wired for peace. If we are worried, frustrated, and think everyone is an enemy, we cannot impart peace. <u>White people are not our enemy</u>. The spirit operating in and through the oppressor, whether the oppressor is black or white, is our enemy.

It is a satanic spirit that divides people, houses, nations, races, and kingdoms.

The peace of God comes only by righteousness. Harmony with God comes through peace, and peace comes by righteousness. We cannot manufacture righteousness in our minds, for our minds do not know the righteousness of God. It is revealed from faith to faith and from grace to grace.

Psalm 72:4 says, **"He shall judge the poor of the people..."** We need to understand that we free God to do some things He has not been able to do in our lives, communities, cities, and nation when there is a continuous standard of righteousness before Him.

God wants us in peace with Him and with each other. If we distrust one another, it is difficult to work together. This is one of the things of our culture that is contrary to righteousness, and it will <u>not</u> exalt a race. To be exalted, repentance must come. There must be a release of those qualities which are contrary to righteousness and peace.

The Lord may ask us to go to a person and ask their forgiveness for something we have said or done. God may identify something we are doing that is working crosswise to His plans and purposes. He may then ask us to get it right. If we do not obey, we fail to be righteous.

When we embrace God's right standing, individually as well as corporately, then the Kingdom of God can flow to us in peace, harmony, and unity.

God wants to establish us in righteousness so He can release His peace to us and through us. He wants us in peace with Him and with one another. A revelation of Jehovah-Shalom (the Lord our peace) was necessary in order for Gideon to be used to deliver Israel from the hand of the Midianites (which means strife, brawling, contentions, discord, contest, or quarrel). The quality of peace is a necessary characteristic in order to war against division, racism, and prejudice. Romans 16:20 justifies this truth: **"And the God of peace shall bruise Satan under your feet..."**

Righteousness Will Release Spiritual Ethiopia's Gifts

Under the inspiration of the Holy Spirit, King Solomon wrote" "...**the kings of Sheba and Seba shall offer gifts**" (Psalm 72:10).

God promises that when He can get us right, He can right the wrongs and release Sheba and let Seba offer her gifts. Seba is a country in the region of Ethiopia that is full of gold.

The treasures of Ethiopia are of renown, but God is not talking about bringing natural gold, because He said, "**The silver is mine, and the gold is mine...**" (Haggai 2:8). He is talking about spiritual Ethiopia, that black faction of the people of God, that has been locked up under oppression...those who have not been accepted by the rest of the Body of Christ and are unable to express themselves. They have not embraced righteousness, and they have not trusted in God.

When we look to God, He will right the wrongs, and He will break the backs of the oppressors (See Psalm 72:4). God wants to lay the axe to the roots. God will stop these inequities. He will stop these imbalances. He will free the Ethiopians to bring their gifts and help the nations. He will free them to bring their spiritual giftings and callings.

Yea, all kings shall fall down before him: all nations shall serve him.

- Psalm 72:11

The inference here is that God will have Sheba bring something that will cause the nations to bow. Why is He talking about the Ethiopian? Why Sheba? Why did God put this verse in the midst of Psalm 72? Why will God release Sheba? Because Sheba had been in bondage; Ethiopia had been in bondage. Ethiopian eunuchs were a part of the Jewish society. God will release those in bondage to bring their gifts or their spiritual deposits, and they will come and have a part in His eternal purposes. This spiritual promise is happening in the natural to the Ethiopians.

Black Christians have something to offer to the Body of Christ. God has put a uniqueness in black Christians. We need to rise up to our destiny. We need to understand and let God judge us. Black Christians must answer the call to consecration in our personal lives as well as corporately. We must let God judge us so we don't miss His day of visitation (See Luke 19:44).

In this way, God will be free to deal with the oppression and will be free to release Sheba and Seba. Black Christians are spiritual Sheba and Seba. God is talking about releasing an oppressed faction. He wants to release the black segment of the Body of Christ - those who have been in servitude and bondage.

The Kingdom of God must be preached and practiced with such intensity, fervor, and drive that not only are we rightly related to God, but we are rightly related to one another. The "one another" is anyone who is blood washed and blood bought.

Righteousness also means the right wisdom of God. Now, in our own wisdom, if someone hurts us, we don't want to forgive them. But the wisdom of God says to forgive. In our own wisdom, if we have a need, we don't want to help someone else. But in God's wisdom, He says, **"Give and it shall be given unto you"** (Luke 6:38).

God's Word says, **"But whoso hath this world's good, and seeth his brother have need, and shutteth up his bowels of compassion from him, how dwelleth the love of God in him?"** (1 John 3:17).

It does not say if you have a need. It says if someone else has a need, don't shut up your bowels of compassion, but give.

God's wisdom is different from man's philosophies and ideologies. God has a wisdom of order, a wisdom of check-points. God has a wisdom of giving His people someone to watch over their souls so we are not caught in the snare of the devil.

The world's wisdom of the hour tells us to be independent, do our own thing, do whatever we feel like doing, and treat people any kind of way. We have to come back under God's wisdom. The Kingdom involves the wisdom of God toward Himself and toward one another - right relationship toward God and right relationship toward one another.

I was educated in our black history in America during the 1960's and 1970's. I personally read almost every book about black history that was written. It did not exalt me. It made me mad. I found out that civil rights and model cities do not exalt a nation. I thought if I got an education, I would be exalted. This is a fallacy, for the Word says that there is only one thing that will exalt you and that is <u>righteousness</u>.

Even though God challenges us as the black segment of the Church, gives us revelation, and tells us His will and desire is to visit us and bring to pass a God-given destiny in our lives, we cannot embrace that on <u>our</u> terms. We must embrace that call on <u>His</u> terms!

God is working in us both to will and to do of His good pleasure (See Philippians 2:13).

For God's Kingdom to come, other kingdoms have to fall. Some kingdoms we don't let go very easily. Everything that rules and reigns over our lives that is not of God, we must let God (the Rock) break in pieces. Any foundation or rule other than Christ must be dug up.

God wants to make all things new, but we have to remember not to hold on to the old. Sometimes God takes the rubble of our lives and makes a new wall and a new temple. Some of us are in the rubbish workshop - becoming new!

So many times the devil puts us in bondage because we have not had very much, and we end up settling for so little. With just the little bit we have, the devil can lure us away and buy us out.

The first requirement of the Kingdom is, "...**Repent: for the kingdom of heaven is at hand**" (Matthew 4:17). God wants to judge us. He wants to judge our habits. He wants to judge our responses to the white segment of society. He wants to judge our responses to our husband or wife. He wants to judge our responses to our brethren. He wants to judge our responses to leaders and those in positions of authority. Judgment always comes to bring forth the righteousness of God.

There is no more time for delay. It is now. Destiny is at hand.

American blacks, because we have been under such pressure and oppression in our own country, we have not been able to rise and answer the call to help other black nations in their time of need. Most blacks know little about what is going on in other countries. Our energies have been exhausted in trying to come out from under all the ropes and weights of oppression.

In Christ Jesus, all of those weights are coming off. A new vision is coming to the black segment of society, which will take our eyes off ourselves and put them on the needs of others. We will see the reality of the Scripture, **"Give, and it shall be given unto you..."** (Luke 6:38). We will also understand that Jesus' consecration was based on His concern for others. He said, **"And for their sakes I sanctify myself..."** (John 17:19).

God truly has raised up the black segment of the Body of Christ **"for such a time as this."**

Chapter 14

Now is God's Time

Dr. Martin Luther King died in hope, not in faith. He died saying that he had seen that it <u>will</u> happen. He saw blacks and whites, Jews and Gentiles, black boys and white boys, black girls and white girls, black women and white women, joining hands and singing the old Negro spiritual, "Free at last, free at last, <u>thank God Almighty</u>, I'm free at last."

He saw it and said, "I will not be there with you, but it will happen." He did not understand the truth of bringing it into a <u>now</u> existence.

The white segment of the Body of Christ in the Spirit-filled ranks had the opportunity in the 1960's to join with Dr. King and right the wrongs that were caused by racism and division. But neither the white nor black segment could, because they were not in right standing with each other. Even though white middle-class America had received a visitation of the Spirit, called the Charismatic renewal, they did not yield to its ministry of bringing us not only in right standing with God, but in right standing with one another.

Previously, we talked about the natural Ethiopians being airlifted to Israel. When they arrived in a setting where they were no longer in bondage and the threat of survival was removed, they were free to advance in the Jewish culture. This was because they were freed of the bondage of the Ethiopian lifestyle. Then they were able to advance socially and cultural-ly in the Jewish lifestyle.

As a black race, we will not progress in the spiritual lifestyle until we get rid of the bondages that smell of the old lifestyle of racism and oppression. There are some things we have to unlearn and some things we have to learn.

Most of the problems among our black brethren around the country are cultural problems. We have the power of God. We have the Word of God. We have the vision of God. We have the anointing of God. We are preaching the message of God. The problem is cultural, both negative and positive.

Culturally, as black people, we have been taught that we are nothing. Our self worth has been little higher than zero on a scale of zero to ten. In understanding that God has given us a destiny, we can eradicate this "nothing" mentality and image of ourselves.

Sometimes we, as a people, do not like to be told anything! We learn a little bit in Bible college, for example, and then want to tell the pastor how to run the church. We need to learn how to receive instructions and submit to divine order and authority. If we are not called to be the leader, then we need to learn how to be followers who can accept instruction. We must get rid of the dislike of being instructed. We must be open to God to judge us in cultural things. God is not going to visit us in our present state. We must change for visitation!

If we allow God to judge us, it frees Him to judge the poor of the people. "**He shall judge the poor of the people, he shall save the children of the needy, and shall break in pieces the oppressor**" (Psalm 72:4). We do not know this nor have we seen Him "Break in pieces the oppressor," because we have never become established in His righteousness.

The message of the Spirit is: <u>As the Spirit moves, He establishes the people in righteousness. He makes them trees of righteousness, symbols of permanence and stability</u>.

God wants us to be righteous continually. He wants us to be an elevator that is continually moving toward Him. We are to be trees of righteousness, "**...the planting of the Lord, that he might be glorified**" (Isaiah 61:3).

Trees are symbols of consistency and permanency. When properly cared for, they last hundreds of years. There have been times of unity and then times of disunity in the church I pastor. Times of high praise and worship and then times of mediocre praise and worship. God is looking for consistency. There have been times of real brotherhood and sisterhood (love and concern for each other), and then times where a selfish spirit has dominated.

When God can get a people into consistent righteousness, they free Him to judge the poor and bring peace. He needs a righteous remnant, because righteousness releases His Kingdom.

God said to me, **"Blacks in America do not believe Me to change a situation. They don't have faith for Me to change things. Their theme song has been, 'We shall overcome someday,' while faith says, 'We overcome now.'"**

Culturally, few blacks received God beyond an emotional feeling, nor did we have faith that God could right the wrongs of society through us. Dr. King admitted that he would not be here to see it happen. Culturally, we were deprived of the God of the now, the God who flattened the walls of Jericho, that calmed the raging sea, that walked the waters of adversity, that miraculously fed the multitude, that raised the dead, that brought healing to sick bodies and destroyed the works of the wicked one.

We needed salvation from the oppressor. We needed salvation from the systems that oppressed us. The Gospel has the power to do that, but we did not believe that it was possible in the now existence. We believed it would be possible later on.

We thought the Word was a storybook, or at least we treated it that way. We had no understanding of Romans 1:16 and 17.

> ...for it [the Gospel] is the power of God unto salvation to every one that believeth; to the Jew first, and also to the Greek.

For therein is the righteousness of God revealed from faith to faith: as it is written, The just shall live by faith.

The black culture was living in hope rather than in faith. The Spirit of God must inspire and bring to life the Word or it is dead. Too many of our black leaders who were fundamentalists were not changed, because they did not know the Spirit. All they knew was the letter, and the letter kills. They did not know the Spirit of the Word becoming alive and present in them. They did not know the Word as a voice, illuminated, revealed, and personal. They did not go out with a Word from God that something was going to happen and then see God fulfill it. They did not understand that until someone believes and proclaims it, it will not happen.

God wants to shine light upon our words and be with our mouth. If all we can say is, "We shall overcome," these are the only words He can move upon. "Shall" is future tense, but God is a God who is a very present help (not a later help) in time of need (See Psalm 46:1).

We have not known how to manifest God to the nations nor how to manifest the God of righteousness in the now. God is raising up a people who have learned to believe Him, to rely on His Word, to stand on His standard of righteousness and proclaim what He says. Faith that is rooted in righteousness functions in the now (See Hebrews 11:1).

God is now ready to right the wrongs, for He is the God of equity and He wants you to know Him in that realm. He is ready to bring the balances now if we can believe it. The righteousness of God is revealed. I like to add, "revealed for the time." If we will embrace it when God says, "This is it," then it shall be.

God is ready now to bring black and white folks together. God wants black folks to get rid of their prejudices, for this is His wisdom. Then if black folks respond, "Well, I'm not fooling around with any whites," we have rejected God's righteousness.

If God says He is ready to right the wrongs and we believe Him and accept it, He will do it. We are sanctified by that truth, and we release God to be whatever He says He is going to be to us and do whatever He says He will do for us. If we do not believe Him, then we do not free Him. It is all tied to embracing righteousness which is revealed now by faith, and faith comes by hearing the Word of God.

God spoke to my heart, "In the Civil Rights Movement, the black culture never believed Me to do anything. They expected that a generation later they would reap the benefits of their protesting today." They did not go out in faith, because faith is now. They did not go out with something already clicking in their spirits with a Word from the Lord. It is God's will to break the oppressor and to judge the poor. Can you believe Him in faith to do it?

God will do it if we can believe it. All changes in us must start in the Spirit. If we get a word from God, it is settled. **"...faith cometh by hearing, and hearing by the word of God"** (Romans 10:17).

When I have a spoken word from God, I am on the right platform for faith, and I have to seal that word by the written Word. If God's voice comes to my heart or speaks to me in the Scriptures saying, "I AM now ready to break the oppressor in pieces, I AM now ready to judge the poor, I AM now ready to save the children of the needy," if I go out in that strength, He will do it. I believe God to change systems now. I believe for it to start in the Spirit.

God said His Church is to become one. He didn't refer to color. We, as believers in the Lord Jesus Christ, whether black, white, red, yellow, or whatever, are to come together as one.

It is a demonic spirit that controls races and causes them to oppress other races of people. That spirit (not people) is our enemy. It is that satanic spirit that separates and divides people, houses, nations, races, and kingdoms. That is our enemy over which we have been given all authority and all power to bind. Now, we must learn how to exercise that authority and power.

Remember, the scriptures say that, "we wrestle not against flesh and blood, but against principalities, against powers, against the rulers of the darkness of this world, against spiritual wickedness in high places." (Ephensians 6:12) I believe that fear and hate are among the rulers of the darkness of this world, and, usually, fear - whether it is of people, races or things - is the foundation upon which hate is built. What we fear - and end up hating - we try to destroy or control. Satan has used fear to put many people in bondage, and "fear hath torment." (I John 4:18) Yet this same scripture says, "...perfect love casteth out fear," love being an attribute of God.

Since hate, bigotry and oppression all have fear as their root, it follows that fear is one of Satan's most powerful tools. That is where our attack must be focused - against fear and the spirit behind it - not against people. This requires us to understand true spiritual warfare and to recognize who it is we are really warring against. When we can see the battle for what it is - spiritual warfare - we will understand that black or white is not the issue. The real issue is the spirit of fear, which Satan, the father of lies, has used to divide races and peoples as it bears it's natural fruit of hatred, bigotry and oppression.

"For God has not given us the spirit of fear; but of power (over the spirit of fear), and of love (God's antidote for fear), and of a sound mind (that will not receive the lies of Satan which produce fear.)" II Tim. 1:7. Here is God's blueprint for fighting racism.

I believe God is ready to bring some of these changes now. I know what is happening in my own born-again spirit. I know that things are happening in others' regenerated spirits right now in relationship to whites and blacks. I am seeing walls fall down spiritually for those who will believe: Walls of division and separation. Walls of hate and prejudice. Walls of fear and intimidation.

As we yield to God and say, "Judge me, Lord...mold me...change me," then we free the God of righteousness and the God of equity to do what is right.

God wants to make a covenant with us. He wants to make a covenant with a people who will hear Him...a people who will embrace righteousness. That's what God meant when He stated in Psalm 72:5, **"They shall fear thee as long as the sun and moon endure, throughout all generations."** This is covenant language. (See Psalm 89:37; Psalm 104:19; Jeremiah 31:31,35-37; Jeremiah 34:20-22,25,26.) He only needs a remnant who will embrace righteousness and right the wrongs. Then He will start judging the poor of the people. He will start saving the children of the needy.

I pray, Lord, break down everything beginning with the devil and every agent working for him. Break those who are oppressing people and keeping them locked into certain lifestyles. Break those who are keeping the black segment of the Body of Christ locked up in ignorance and a lack of intelligence, causing them to believe they have no hope. God, we are asking You to break the oppressor. We are not saying for You to break black or white folks. But we are saying, "Break the oppressor." Whatever the <u>root</u> of the oppression is, break it in Jesus' name. Whatever the spirit behind the oppression, we bind it now in Jesus' name, causing it to desist in its maneuvers from this day forth and forever.

This is an ongoing prophetic challenge, prayer, and call to the black segment of the Body of Christ.

God is ready to visit the black segment of the Body of Christ if we are ready to receive. This is God's word and challenge to our generation. **<u>If we will embrace righteousness, God will free us as a nation of black people</u>.**

Bibliography

Bent, J. Theodore. The Sacred City of the Ethiopians, London: Longmans, Green and Company, 1983.

Clarke, John Henrik. "Africa in Early World History," Ebony Magazine, Chicago: Johnson Publishing Company, August, 1976.

Combined Bible Dictionary and Concordance (The New), Grand Rapids: Baker Book House, Reprint, 1985.

Freeman, James M. Manners and Customs of the Bible, Plainfield: Logos International, 1972.

Halley, Henry M. Halley's Bible Handbook, Grand Rapids: Zondervan Publishing House, 1965.

Holly, Alonzo Potter. God and the Negro, Nashville: National Baptist Publishing Board, 1937.

Hyman, Mark. Blacks Who Died for Jesus, Philadelphia: Corrective Black History Books, 1983.

Hyman, Mark. 150 Facts About Blacks, Philadelphia: Mark Hyman Associates, Inc.

International Standard Bible Encyclopedia, Vol. 2, Grand Rapids: Wm. B. Eerdmans, 1956.

Jones, A. H. M. & Elizabeth Monroe, A History of Abyssinia, Oxford: Clarendon Press, 1935.

King James Version of the Bible (The).

Lockyer, Herbert. All the Men of the Bible, Grand Rapids: Zondervan Publishing House, 1958.

Lockyer, Herbert. All the Women of the Bible, Grand Rapids: Zondervan Publishing House, 1967.

Mitchell, Thurman. Personal Interview & Video from trip to Israel Observing Airlifted Ethiopian Jews, Kansas City, 1986.

Reader's Digest. <u>Atlas of the Bible</u>, Pleasantville: Reader's Digest Association, Inc., 1981.

Rhoades, F. S. <u>Black Characters and References of the Holy Bible</u>, New York: Vantage Press, Inc., 1980.

Safran, Claire. "Secret Exodus: The Story of Operation Moses from a Forthcoming Book," <u>Reader's Digest</u>, Pleasantville: Reader's Digest Association, Inc., January, 1987.

Strong, James H. <u>Strong's Exhaustive Concordance</u>, Grand Rapids: Baker Book House, Reprint, 1985.

Unger, Merrill F. & William White, Jr. <u>Nelson's Expository Dictionary of the Old Testament</u>, Nashville: Thomas Nelson Publishers, 1980.

Unger, Merrill F. <u>Unger's Bible Dictionary</u>, Chicago: Moody Press, 1973.

Vine, W. E. & F. F. Bruce. <u>Vine's Expository Dictionary of Old and New Testament Words</u>, Old Tappen: Fleming H. Revell Company, 1981.

Woolsey, Raymond H. <u>Men and Women of Color in the Bible</u>, Langley Park: International Bible, Inc., 1977.

Yeshag. "Glory of the Kings" in <u>Kebra Nagast</u>, London: Oxford University Press, 1932.